The Demands of Discipleship

THE DEMANDS OF DISCIPLESHIP

Expository Messages from Daniel

Michael A. Milton, Ph. D.

Wipf and Stock Publishers
Eugene, Oregon

Wipf and Stock Publishers
199 W 8th Ave, Suite 3
Eugene, OR 97401

The Demands of Discipleship
Expository Messages from Daniel
By Milton, Michael A.
Copyright©2005 by Milton, Michael A.
ISBN: 1-59752-217-1
Publication date 5/25/2005

Unless otherwise indicated, all Scripture quotations are from The Holy Bible, English Standard Version, copyright © 2001 by Crossway Bibles, a division of Good News Publishers. Used by permission. All rights reserved.

1st edition.

Dedication

"Of all of the truths I've been told
There's none that more soothes my soul
Than knowing that God's in control
It gives me the strength to go on…"

Lord Jesus Christ, I wrote those words as a testimony to the divine disclosure You gave me about the wonder of Your sovereignty. I can't get over You! I commend this little volume to You and Your secret purposes and to the glory of Your sovereign grace, which saved this filthy sinner who is unworthy to even speak Your holy name, much less preach Your Son's glorious gospel!

Thank you my Sovereign Father. Thank you.

And I dedicate this to my earthly father
Jessie Ellis Milton
Who understood the writing on the wall and fled
to the True King
Just in time.

And always for my Mae.

Contents

	Acknowledgments	i
	Introduction	iii
Chapter 1	Discipleship in Babylon	7
Chapter 2	Realizing Your Destiny in Unexpected Places	23
Chapter 3	Facing the Fire and Living with Lions	39
Chapter 4	A Night to Remember	55
Chapter 5	The Relationship of Prophecy and Missions	69
	Author Biography	83

Acknowledgments

As a parish minister, laboring however ingloriously between staff meetings, budget presentations, counseling appointments, committee business, Word, sacrament and prayer, this kind of writing ministry is possible only through the faithful (often unnoticed and, even worse, unthanked) efforts of very dedicated and understanding people. I wish to thank my session for their prayers; my executive pastor, The Reverend Steve Wallace, for his constant labors (to me and to our staff and our congregation); my secretary Mrs. Martha Miller for her servant-like spirit; Mrs. Joye Howard for her expert preparation of the manuscript; our deacons for their concern to lend tithes and offerings to this kind of ministry; and our congregation, First Presbyterian Church of Chattanooga, Tennessee. After Christ and my family, I love this place where God has called me greatly.

Every sermon here reproduced started in the presence of a congregation of two: John Michael Ellis Milton, my son, and Mae Milton, my wife. I love you. I thank you. I just couldn't do it without you. Thanks for the late Saturday nights when you fell asleep as I read the manuscript and then woke up as sudden silence ended my monotone reading to say, through the blur of oncoming sleep, "Dad, that was just great." Your love is precious.

We have sought to document all creative references in these messages. Occasionally, documentation of illustrations that were found in others' messages have been omitted if I found them undocumented in several sermons. But if someone should find that credit is due and has been overlooked, please let me know.

The ministry of Wipf and Stock Publishers of Eugene, Oregon, allows the messages heard on Sunday mornings at our church to be put into print. In this, they are colaborers in the gospel.

INTRODUCTION

The book of Daniel has often been used to study prophecy. This is a good and worthy study, and a study on the book of Daniel will surely yield intellectually stimulating results. (It has also led to some strong disagreements by people who might otherwise agree about everything else!) But the object of my concern in this series of messages, preached in the Autumn of 2004 before my congregation at First Presbyterian Church of Chattanooga, Tennessee, was to locate the gospel in Daniel that would lead us to become faithful followers of Jesus Christ in our generation—a place that is not unlike Babylon. I set out to accomplish this goal within a limited amount of time. I wanted to throw my line in, stay out of the prophetic weeds of this great book which threatened to snag my pastoral purposes, and try to land God's good expositive truths that would feed us with a faith for living. A pastor may, of course (indeed, should at some time), move verse-by-verse through a book, dealing with the hard things, wrestling—even before the congregation—with difficulties and perplexing prophecies. I say again, this is a good and worthy goal. But I chose to preach these five messages on Daniel and have our people leave saying, "Christ is with me, right where I am…in my Babylon." In other words, I see Daniel as *Every Believer*. I see Babylon as *the place of our exile*. The sovereign God of Daniel, who stood in opposition to the gods of Babylon, to the powers of a great worldly empire, is the same sovereign God who stands with the disciples of Jesus against the gods of this age and powers of our world today. He stands with the child of God today as He stood with Daniel. My heart, as a pastor, longs for you to know that He stands with you.

I pray that God will use these few messages from this great book to bless you. Jesus said, "I will never leave you nor forsake you." I believe that through the truths of Daniel, you may know His presence and power in your life. If one thought from these little homilies is used by our kind Savior to disclose Himself to you, in your life, your challenges—your *Babylon*—then the effort to record these words will be more than worth it.

Christ is with you!

Michael A. Milton

Pentecost, 2005

"The principal theological emphasis in Daniel is the absolute sovereignty of Yahweh, the God of Israel."

Gleason L. Archer

"Beloved brethren…God proves the faith of His people in these days by various trials; and…with wonderful wisdom He has taken care to strengthen their minds by ancient examples, that they should never be weakened by the concussion of the severest storms and tempests; or at least, if they should totter at all, that they should never finally fall away."

John Calvin

1

DISCIPLESHIP IN BABYLON

Daniel 1

I love travel books. Whether it is John Steinbeck's *Travels with Charlie* or just a second-hand book I picked up yesterday at an antique store in Red Bank, I love to read travel books. They are guides to places I have never been, or when they are really good, they are insights into things I see all the time, but I get to see them in a new way.

The Lord led me to this book of Daniel for our new fall series. The book of Daniel is a divine travel guide for pilgrims who are passing through Babylon. The six stories and four dreams that make up this apocalyptic book of the Old Testament are many things to us.

- They are clearly prophetic. Daniel prophesies the coming of Christ down to the year. Daniel prophesies the kingdoms of the Medes, Persians, Alexander the Great and his successor, Rome. He paves the way for a fifth monarchy which will be out of this world and will never go away, clearly showing the birth and growth of the kingdom of God through Jesus Christ. Daniel prophesies desolations, and Daniel prophesies deliverance. Some wonder whether Daniel is just an allegory written by a later scribe seeking to encourage faith in the Jews. But in Matthew 24:15 Jesus Christ says that Daniel is a prophet. So this book, placed between the Major Prophets and the Minor Prophets, is in a perfect place. Yes, surely, this is, like the book of Revelation, an apocalyptic book describing what will happen. And like Revelation, it is more.
- Daniel is a great theological book. The subject of Daniel is not Daniel, nor is it Nebuchadnezzar the king. The proper subject of Daniel is God. And the late great Old Testament scholar, Gleason Archer, had it absolutely right when he summarized this book, "The principal theological emphasis in Daniel is the absolute sovereignty of Yahweh, the God of Israel."[1] And

---

[1] Gleason Archer, "Daniel" in Frank E. Gaebelein, ed, *The Expositor's Bible Commentary*, vol 7 (Grand Rapids, Michigan: Zondervan Publishing House, 1985), 8.

one cannot approach this book without coming into contact with the mystery and the glory and the certain reality of Almighty God ruling and reigning, even through evil kings, over all of mankind.

- But the book of Daniel is the place where prophecy and theology meet in a teenage boy named Daniel in captivity to a foreign king. Along with Daniel's friends, the reader comes face-to-face with the realities in his own life:
  ◦ How a believer must live in times of apostasy
  ◦ How a believer may follow the Lord in the most secular of conditions
  ◦ How a follower of Christ can trust Christ even when it seems He is not in control
  ◦ How a disciple of Jesus can meet the demands of discipleship in the tough, hard places of life

As your pastor, this part of Daniel grips me. So I am back to why I love travel books. Think of Daniel as your divine guide to living for God in those times when it looks like God is nowhere to be found. And if we are truly becoming the secular nation that many say we are, then Daniel is God's guide for our lives as we stand up for Him in this generation. With this introduction to the series "The Demands of Discipleship," let us read Daniel 1.

> In the third year of the reign of Jehoiakim king of Judah, Nebuchadnezzar king of Babylon came to Jerusalem and besieged it. And the Lord gave Jehoiakim king of Judah into his hand, with some of the vessels of the house of God. And he brought them to the land of Shinar, to the house of his god, and placed the vessels in the treasury of his god. Then the king commanded Ashpenaz, his chief eunuch, to bring some of the people of Israel, both of the royal family and of the nobility, youths without blemish, of good appearance and skillful in all wisdom, endowed with knowledge, understanding learning, and competent to stand in the king's palace, and to teach them the literature and language of the Chaldeans. The king assigned them a daily portion of the food that the king ate, and of the wine that he drank. They were to be educated for three years, and at the end of that time they were to stand before the king. Among these were Daniel, Hananiah, Mishael, and Azariah of the tribe of Judah. And the chief of the eunuchs gave them names: Daniel he called Belteshazzar, Hananiah he called Shadrach, Mishael he called Meshach, and Azariah he called Abednego. But Daniel resolved that he would not defile himself with the king's food, or with the wine that he drank. Therefore he asked the chief of the eunuchs to allow him not to defile himself. And God gave Daniel favor and compassion in the sight of the chief of the eunuchs, and the chief of the eunuchs said to Daniel, "I fear my lord the king, who assigned your food and your drink; for why should he see that you were in worse condition than the youths who are of your own age? So you

would endanger my head with the king." Then Daniel said to the steward whom the chief of the eunuchs had assigned over Daniel, Hananiah, Mishael, and Azariah, "Test your servants for ten days; let us be given vegetables to eat and water to drink. Then let our appearance and the appearance of the youths who eat the king's food be observed by you, and deal with your servants according to what you see." So he listened to them in this matter, and tested them for ten days. At the end of ten days it was seen that they were better in appearance and fatter in flesh than all the youths who ate the king's food. So the steward took away their food and the wine they were to drink, and gave them vegetables. As for these four youths, God gave them learning and skill in all literature and wisdom, and Daniel had understanding in all visions and dreams. At the end of the time, when the king had commanded that they should be brought in, the chief of the eunuchs brought them in before Nebuchadnezzar. And the king spoke with them, and among all of them none was found like Daniel, Hananiah, Mishael, and Azariah. Therefore they stood before the king. And in every matter of wisdom and understanding about which the king inquired of them, he found them ten times better than all the magicians and enchanters that were in all his kingdom. And Daniel was there until the first year of King Cyrus. (Daniel 1:1-21)

How Do I Follow God in a Place Like This?

It was summer of 1994. I sat with Billy, a new inmate at Leavenworth Penitentiary, in the quiet chapel of the famous military prison. He was a "fresh one." I can remember that the only sound I could hear in that moment was an air conditioner churning out cold air on that hot Kansas day. Billy was a young enlisted man in the Navy but was now wearing the unmistakable dungaree uniform that told the world he was an inmate. I spoke to him as his head was hanging low. "Why are you here, son?" I asked. "Well, I needed money. We were in the midst of an adoption. The baby was soon to come. Now I won't see her…" He began to sob. "Go on, Billy." "We needed money. I was—am—in debt. I passed a BMW and somehow my eyes were drawn to look inside. I would have never done that before, but this time I did. I wish I had never…" "Go on, Bill…" I prodded. "Well, there was a wallet on the seat. I have no idea why, but all of a sudden I got this rush all through my body and I just took a rock and I broke the window and I got the wallet and ran. Would you believe it?" He smiled, and I could tell that he was trying to add some evasive humor. "Would you believe it? I broke into the commander's car." We talked about the process Billy went through and how he got from that moment to Leavenworth. "The question now is, What will I do with my life? You see, Chaplain, I want to follow the Lord. But how do I follow Him in a place like this?"

That last question—How do I follow the Lord in a place like this?—is a question on many minds. We are not in Leavenworth, but all of us are in a similar place.

Last week we talked of the need for revival in our nation. We are in a dry and thirsty land where to stand up for Christ risks alienation from people at work and school. That place has a name.

I know of husbands and wives and even children who must live out their faith in Christ in homes where there is either disdain or disregard from the things of God. That place has a name.

I know of students in universities who must stand their ground in a trial pitting their faith in Jesus Christ against atheistic professors who see themselves as bastions of enlightenment obligated to liberate these poor young people from the chains of religion. Their answer to his essay question will determine their final grade. That place has a name.

I know of people who have been faithful to God and are now facing life-and-death illnesses, and the urge to join Job's wife and curse God and die is all too real. That place has a name.

What is that name? That place of exile, that place of loneliness, that place of testing is a place called Babylon.

Babylon was the place of captivity for God's people, including a young man named Daniel. After warnings of coming judgment, God used the powerful armies of Nebuchadnezzar of Babylon to attack Jerusalem. About 100 years after the Northern Kingdom of Israel fell to Assyria, the powerful and ruthless army of the Chaldeans under mighty King Nebuchadnezzar assaulted Jerusalem in 605 B.C. and again in 597 B.C. when King Jehoiakim was taken into captivity. Finally, after an insurrection, Nebuchadnezzar's army not only crushed the rebellion but also completely destroyed the city of David. Jeremiah records the awful scene in Lamentations. God's people, the great and the small, those who hated God, those who didn't believe in God, those who believed in Him but didn't follow Him, and those who were faithful, were then carried off into exile. For seventy years, the people of God would have to follow God, trust in God, and worship God as His people in a foreign land. Babylon became the dividing line in Israel's history. Just as we say B.C. and A.D. when speaking of human history, we speak of pre-exilic and post-exilic (pre-exile to Babylon and post-exile to Babylon) when speaking of the history of Israel. Even the birth narratives of Jesus mention Babylon. But in the Bible, Babylon is not only that place where Nimrod sought to build a tower to reach to heaven; it is not only the place where God dispersed mankind by dividing them into different languages; it is not only the capitol of the Chaldean Empire in ancient Mesopotamia (modern day Iraq); Babylon is not only a real place for Daniel; but in the Bible, Babylon is a metaphor for every group, every condition that threatens faith in God's people. Thus, in 1 Peter 5:13, Peter will speak of writing from Babylon, though presumably he was really writing from Rome. In Revelation, the Lord speaks of the final enemies of Christ as Babylon.

The place where our faith is under attack, the place of antagonism for the gospel, the place to which we are led that seems alien to our faith—that is Babylon.

But the good news of Daniel is that God is also in Babylon. God is in the hard places of life. God is in the prison with you. God is in the antagonistic classroom with you. God is in the wicked workplace. God is in the unbelieving home. And in Daniel God doesn't minimize the pain of Babylon; He reveals it as it is.

In Daniel 1 we learn five lessons about what discipleship in Babylon is all about.

Discipleship in Babylon—A frightening place where the enemies of God encircle you (Daniel 1:1)

In the third year of the reign of Jehoiakim king of Judah, Nebuchadnezzar king of Babylon came to Jerusalem and besieged it (Daniel 1:1).

I am gripped by the word "besieged." It is the Hebrew verb (*tsur*) meaning, "to siege, besiege, enclose." Slowly but surely, Judah had wandered from God (not Daniel, but his nation) until one day the enemy encircled them. Through no fault of his own, Daniel was also encircled. To follow the Lord now was to follow Him in the presence of enemies. Gleason Archer noted that this whole book of Daniel is about God's sovereignty. God's sovereignty has led you to live before the Lord in the presence of enemies.

Is this not what David wrote of when he composed that beautiful Psalm which we sang today?

> Thou preparest a table before me in the presence of mine enemies...
> (Psalms 23:5, KJV).

That is Babylon. But that is where faith in Christ must be lived out.

I cannot think of the enemy encircling us without thinking of an incident I have mentioned before. Colonel Roger Ingalvson ejected from his plane in Vietnam and was surprised that he had actually survived the ejection only to float down in that parachute and be encircled by the enemy. For Roger that would be the beginning of a new life: a free stay at the Hanoi Hilton, which no words can describe and for which no country can fully repay for the pain endured for being an American. But that prison was also the beginning of a new life of faith in Jesus Christ. His first year was in solitary confinement. He learned how to examine the parts of a bug's body and thank God for His creation. He learned to pray. He remembered the Scriptures he had been taught as a young boy in a Lutheran church in Minnesota. Roger was encircled by an enemy. But Roger would tell you that as the Vietcong encircled him, God encircled him as well.

Discipleship is not always as clean as we would like it. But if our goal is to grow in the grace and knowledge of Christ, and if God is in control, then we can trust that He knows what He is doing. We can believe that even when we have been encircled by Babylonians, God is there. And if we are His, then we can trust Him. We can know that He intends for us to follow Him through it all.

In Daniel, there must be a generation that would do that. One day there would be a revival of true faith. One day there would be a rebuilding of the temple. One day there would be a renewed passion for God. Therefore, God must raise up Daniels.

And that may be what God is doing in your life. Remember the old hymn and apply the truths to your life:

> God moves in a mysterious way
> His wonders to perform,
> He plants his footsteps in the sea,
> And rides upon the storm.
>
> Ye fearful saints, fresh courage take;
> The clouds ye so much dread
> Are big with mercy and shall break
> In blessings on your head.

Today maybe you feel like you are being encircled by things that frighten you, disturb you. My beloved, behind those Babylonian soldiers you are facing in your world, is the invisible hand of your heavenly Father. You will learn to trust the Lord more there than at any other time.

Discipleship in Babylon—A foreign land where God leads us (Daniel 1:2)

> And the Lord gave Jehoiakim king of Judah into his hand, with some of the vessels of the house of God. And he brought them to the land of Shinar, to the house of his god, and placed the vessels in the treasury of his god (Daniel 1:2).

The beginning of Daniel shows that he was not only a captive of Nebuchadnezzar, but that God was in it. The Bible in no way tries to soften the blow of God's sovereignty. It leaves us, always, with the great question of the ages, Why would God allow this to happen?

One of the most amazing passages in the Bible is in the beginning of the Gospel of Mark:

> In those days Jesus came from Nazareth of Galilee and was baptized by John in the Jordan. And when he came up out of the water, immediately he saw the heavens opening and the Spirit descending on him like a dove. And a voice came from heaven, "You are my beloved Son; with you I am well pleased." **The Spirit immediately drove him out into the wilderness.** And he was in the wilderness forty days, being tempted by Satan. And he was with the wild animals, and the angels were ministering to him (Mark 1:9-13).

I emphasize the words "The Spirit immediately **drove** Him out into the wilderness" because only Mark states it like this. Matthew and Luke say, "The Spirit led him," but Mark says, "The Spirit drove him." Mark, as always, just puts it out there in the hardest possible theological language for you and me to deal with.

This is what is going on here. Jeremiah had been prophesying about this. Now it had come. God had caused a heathen nation to come against the people of God and to take them into a foreign land. Now, God is not the author of sin, and God is good. Yet, this was a bad day in Israel's history.

The baptism of Jesus was good. The Father and the Son and the Holy Spirit are one; yet, the third person of the Trinity, we are told, drives the second person of the Trinity into the wilderness to be tempted by Satan, to be subject to wild animals.

No resolution of the mystery is given in Daniel or in Mark. We are told this so that we can see that God is in control and not absent even as we are being led away.

A young pastor, recently called to an older congregation, was called to the bedside of a dying parishioner. The lady was a godly woman who had served the Lord all of her life. Suddenly, she was experiencing heart failure. The family was told that their loved one had only days to live. As the young pastor stood with the family and as he recognized that everyone seemed to be looking to him for words, he froze. All of his theology and Bible study and pastoral training suddenly stuck in his throat. He finally managed a word, but it would have been better left unsaid. "Ma'am, this is not of God. God is not in this." The dying saint raised her head with all of the strength she had left. "Pastor, if God is not in this, then I am lost. My God is right here in all of it. God led me to this place. But don't worry, Pastor. I love the Lord Jesus, and I trust Him with my life." The pastor never made that mistake again.

God leads us to places that are foreign to us so that we can trust Him. In some mysterious way—and you cannot read Daniel without acknowledging mystery—we come to know His love greater in Babylon.

Discipleship in Babylon—An intimidating place where we are under the power of an antagonist (Daniel 1:3-7)

In Daniel 1:3-7, the young man Daniel (James Boice supposes him to be between fifteen and seventeen years old) and his friends are put in the royal court. They were members of the ruling class of Judah. They were strong, bright young men; and the king wanted to bring them into his religion, into his culture, and to thoroughly indoctrinate them for further service in his kingdom. Not only will they have to take a stand for their faith, they will have to do so under extremely antagonistic conditions. So Ashpenaz, the king's chief eunuch, changes their names:

> And the chief of the eunuchs gave them names: Daniel he called Belteshazzar, Hananiah he called Shadrach, Mishael he called Meshach, and Azariah he called Abednego (Daniel 1:7).

Let's look at this for a moment.

The name change is important because each of the young men's names contains elements of God's name. Daniel and Mishael both contain the "el" as in Elohim, the frequently used name for God. Daniel means "God is my Judge." Mishael means "Who is like God?" Hananiah and Azariah "contain a shortened form of the name Jehovah." Hananiah means "Jehovah is gracious." Azariah means "Jehovah is my helper." Thus these young men took the testimony of God with them wherever they went in their very names. The chief eunuch gave them new names and the names he gave them all had "a reference to one of the false gods of the ancient Babylonians: Aku and Nego. But as Jim Boice put it, "Nebuchadnezzar changed the men's names, but he could not change their hearts."[2]

And this is the very thing we must see. The outward situation for these young men changed, but their true identity was unchanged.

I talk to people who say, "I don't understand why God put me under this boss. He doesn't know the Lord." Or, "Why the Lord put me in this place that is so ungodly, I will never know." You may never know why, but you are there. But what is more important, He is there. If your identity is in Christ, it doesn't matter if you are in Babylon or where. The truth is that you carry Christ with you wherever you go.

Discipleship in Babylon—A testing place where true holiness is defined (Daniel 1:8-16)

You know the story. These young men are told to eat the king's food and drink the king's drink. The reasons are not completely clear in the text, but since it says that Daniel refused to defile himself, it is likely that the food had been offered to Babylonian idols. Daniel's faith was now on trial. That is what happens in Babylon, in tough times, in hard times, in places where God is mocked.

I told you last week about returning from Britain with a burden. That burden will not be lifted in my heart until I see revival in America. But this I can tell you: in Britain today, there are not many middle-of-the-road Christians. You are with God or you with the world. If our nation continues on its slide toward Gomorrah, then this will become our Babylon and our nation will become a place where true holiness is defined.

True holiness is a life consumed with the love of God in Christ. True holiness is not religiosity or a goody-two-shoes holiness. That kind of pseudo-holiness cannot withstand the heat of the wilderness or the temptations of Babylon. That kind of holiness cannot withstand the promise of greatness that will come if only you will consume the idolatrous food and drink, if only you will bend the knee.

I heard from a soldier who recently went to battle in Iraq. I heard him say that it is when you are moving through the war-torn, insurgent-infested rubble of

---

[2] James Montgomery Boice, *Daniel: An Expositional Commentary* (Grand Rapids, Michigan: Baker Books, 1989), 21.

Fallujah that you come to understand what you and your unit are really made of.

As a businessman, I remember that true holiness was defined, not on Sunday morning, but in the workweek when decisions had to be made that involved living for Christ, when being called to join the crowd and live like He wasn't there. True faith is defined when you are out of town and all day meetings turn into all night partying, and you are faced with following Christ or compromising, risking alienation from your boss who grades your performance or assuring isolation from the Lord who loves you.

Maybe you are where you are right now, beloved, to prove the metal of your faith, to determine whether your holiness is a religious, man-centered legalism or a heart constrained by the love of Jesus Christ. As Bryan Chapell said:

> "We resolve to remain undefiled for the sake of Jesus, who washes us with his blood and holds us in his love."[3]

Discipleship in Babylon—A sacred place where others become disciples (Daniel 1:17-21)

At the conclusion of this story, Daniel chose a simple diet, chose an honorable way to be obedient to his new authority and to honor God. The Bible says that God will honor those who honor Him. Listen to what happened in the court of the Babylonian king:

> As for these four youths, God gave them learning and skill in all literature and wisdom, and Daniel had understanding in all visions and dreams. At the end of the time, when the king had commanded that they should be brought in, the chief of the eunuchs brought them in before Nebuchadnezzar. And the king spoke with them, and among all of them none was found like Daniel, Hananiah, Mishael, and Azariah. Therefore they stood before the king. And in every matter of wisdom and understanding about which the king inquired of them, he found them ten times better than all the magicians and enchanters that were in all his kingdom (Daniel 1:17-20).

The testimony of Daniel was established. The rest of this book will tell how God used this lad to speak to a heathen nation, to show God's sovereignty over all things, to prophecy concerning Jesus Christ, and to establish the lordship of Christ in human history. But it started with a small act of obedience.

---

[3] Bryan Chapell, *Standing Your Ground: A Call to Courage in an Age of Compromise: Messages from Daniel* (Grand Rapids, Michigan: Baker Book House, 1989), 37.

When that happens, we become living testimonies for God. In the very hard places of life where we are led, the mysterious places where we don't understand why the innocent suffer or why we suffer—it is in those places where small decisions are made to trust Christ regardless; it is in those places that we become living testimonies for others. Daniel had to be a testimony for those three young men. Every Sunday school child knows that Shadrach, Meshack, and Abednego were going to have a challenge. But would they ever forget the strength of Daniel. Nebuchadnezzar would know the strength of Daniel. They would all know the power of God at work in one teen-age boy who overflowed with the love of God in his heart.

We see that this evil place, this place of paganism, became, for one tried and true young man, a place where other disciples were made. Daniel was a great evangelist; yet, he was in a foreign land. Daniel was a great theologian who taught others about God; yet, he was a slave. Daniel was a leader; yet, Daniel was just a lad. In Babylon, Daniel stirred up the faith of his friends who would later need strong faith themselves. And he witnessed to a pagan king.

This reminds me of Paul in prison in Rome. He wrote to the Philippians to encourage them about his situation.

> I want you to know, brothers, that what has happened to me has really served to advance the gospel, so that it has become known throughout the whole imperial guard and to all the rest that my imprisonment is for Christ (Philippians 1:12-13).

Through faith in Christ, the hard places of life become sacred places.

You wouldn't believe that cancer is a sacred place. The mere mention of the word makes us stop, like someone suddenly hearing a rattler and a hiss. But as awful as such a place is, I have witnessed sacred places in such times. A friend of mine is in a heroic fight with cancer. I talked to his wife on the telephone the other night, and she told me about how my friend came to view the awful menace facing him. When the doctor broke the news of an inoperable cancer, in a way it was like Jerusalem falling; it was like being led away to Babylon. She said that at the moment he came to understand what he was facing, it was as if God put His arm around her husband, and from that time on, the man of God she had known showed a depth of discipleship that she could never have imagined. I have talked to this man and prayed with him. His wife is not exaggerating. His faith is amazing. And hers is as well.

I cannot tell you why Jerusalem fell and captivity came to a faithful man like Daniel except that there was evil in the land. I cannot tell you why good men of God like my friend, and some of you, get cancer except that there is evil in this world. But this I know: in Babylon Daniel's faith led others to trust in God. And I have seen how others are affected by the suffering of a Spirit-controlled saint of God.

We don't want to go to Babylon, and we don't pray for anyone to go to Babylon, but Babylons happen in this life. The question is, Where is the power for you to go through Babylon? The answer is in the one who came from heaven to His Babylon—the manger, the cross, the tomb were Babylon. Jesus Christ identified with us in the hardest places of life—in fact, in places we will never go. He took upon Himself the shame and condemnation of the cross that He might identify with us, that we may know that He is with us in Babylon.

Conclusion

Babylon is not where we want to be. But sometimes in life it is where we end up. So today we have learned

- Discipleship in Babylon is a frightening place where the enemies of God encircle you (Daniel 1:1)
- Discipleship in Babylon is a foreign land where God leads us (Daniel 1:2)
- Discipleship in Babylon is an intimidating place where we are under the power of an antagonist (Daniel 1:3-7)
- Discipleship in Babylon is a testing place where true holiness is defined (Daniel 1:8-16)
- Discipleship in Babylon is a sacred place where others become disciples (Daniel 1:17-21)

The last time I saw Billy at Leavenworth was on one of the final pastoral rounds I made there. I will never forget it. I was drawn to whistling coming from one of the cellblocks You have heard about a caged bird singing, but this was too bizarre to be real. Whistling in Leavenworth is like giggling in Dante's *Inferno* and is not something you hear everyday. But there he was. It was Billy, the young Navy lad I had interviewed when he first came. He was happier than I was. In fact he almost glowed with joy. Billy had a broom and was sweeping the hall just outside his cell, and he was whistling as he swept. I was inspired by his cheerfulness myself. He was so into his sweeping and whistling that I startled him when I approached and asked, "Billy, how's it going?" "Well, Chaplain, I am doing just fine!" He was smiling ear to ear. "Billy, it looks like you have learned how to live in this place." "Chaplain, what I have found is that Jesus can live this for me. Jesus is here in this cell. I am going to learn more about Him and learn to follow Him like never before. This is not a cell; this is my school of faith. Come look at the picture of my wife and daughter, Chaplain...."

You see, the truth of the book of Daniel is that the love of a sovereign God knows no boundaries. He is the God named Jesus who comes to our Babylon and turns a place of exile into a sanctuary. Jesus comes to our Babylon in a manger, on a cross, through an empty tomb, through the Holy Spirit. And He lives in our hearts wherever we are.

Where is your Babylon? And how are you doing there? Complaining? Giving in? Or trusting? And where is your power coming from? Do I again hear whistling in the cell? Or is it the quiet voice of a gentle Savior saying, "I am here."

As your pastor, I was so taken by this book and your lives testifying to me, that I wrote a song. I will sing the refrain.

> And He was there in the fire
> He was there in the Lion's den
> He was there working all things together
> For good to those who love Him
> And are called by Him
> And that gives me hope
> For my lifeFor he is there in my sorrow
> He is there in my physical pain
> He is there in the sunshine of life
> And He's there in the seasons of rain
> He is there

Questions for Reflection

1. Daniel is the story of a faithful disciple being called to a difficult place. Has God called you to a difficult place in your life? How can you serve God in your Babylon?

2. How can God use His enemies to produce faithfulness in His people?

3. Where are the circumstantial testing places you are facing in your life today? How is God using these circumstances to build your faith?

4. If God has put you in a difficult place in your life, who are the people around you? Take some time to study the life of Paul in Philippians. Study the first chapter and the last chapter of that book. How did God use Paul's Babylon to reach others? What does this say about how God may be working in the post-Christian West today? Or in China or India?

Prayer

Sovereign Lord, your love and wisdom transcend my circumstance. But my vision is limited. My faith is often weak. I plead for you to strengthen my love and trust in You for the places where I live today. In the name of Your Son, my Savior, Jesus Christ.

"The grand design of God in all afflictions that befall His people is to bring them nearer and closer to Himself."

Thomas Brooks

"The whole of life is a test, a trial of what is in us, so arranged by God himself."

William S. Plumer

2

REALIZING YOUR DESTINY IN UNEXPECTED PLACES

Daniel 2:1-5, 11-24; 4:13-25, 33-37

You expect God in majestic cathedrals, in the quiet abbeys of a monastery, or in an evangelical crusade. But how about in the wonders of a polar bear or in the plays of Shakespeare? Philip Yancy's *Finding God in Unexpected Places*[1] is a book that proposes that the footprints of God may be found in the most surprising places, if you have eyes to see.

Another proposition from the Bible might be, Finding God's will for your life in unexpected places. The purposes of God may be also found in surprising places.

God's will for Daniel's life, his destiny, would be found when his life comes into contact with a ruthless dictator and his troubled dreams. How many here are looking for God's will? Are you looking in the right places? Is His will really right in front of you?

> In the second year of the reign of Nebuchadnezzar, Nebuchadnezzar had dreams; his spirit was troubled, and his sleep left him. Then the king commanded that the magicians, the enchanters, the sorcerers, and the Chaldeans be summoned to tell the king his dreams. So they came in and stood before the king. And the king said to them, "I had a dream, and my spirit is troubled to know the dream." Then the Chaldeans said to the king in Aramaic, "O king, live forever! Tell your servants the dream, and we will show the interpretation." The king answered and said to the Chaldeans, "The word from me is firm: if you do not make known to me the dream and its interpretation, you shall be torn limb from limb, and your houses shall be laid in ruins. (Daniel 2:1-5)

---

[1] Philip Yancey, *Finding God in Unexpected Places*, (New York, NY: Doubleday & Company, 2005).

The thing that the king asks is difficult, and no one can show it to the king except the gods, whose dwelling is not with flesh." Because of this the king was angry and very furious, and commanded that all the wise men of Babylon be destroyed. So the decree went out, and the wise men were about to be killed; and they sought Daniel and his companions, to kill them. Then Daniel replied with prudence and discretion to Arioch, the captain of the king's guard, who had gone out to kill the wise men of Babylon. He declared to Arioch, the king's captain, "Why is the decree of the king so urgent?" Then Arioch made the matter known to Daniel. And Daniel went in and requested the king to appoint him a time, that he might show the interpretation to the king. Then Daniel went to his house and made the matter known to Hananiah, Mishael, and Azariah, his companions, and told them to seek mercy from the God of heaven concerning this mystery, so that Daniel and his companions might not be destroyed with the rest of the wise men of Babylon. Then the mystery was revealed to Daniel in a vision of the night. Then Daniel blessed the God of heaven. Daniel answered and said: "Blessed be the name of God forever and ever, to whom belong wisdom and might. He changes times and seasons; he removes kings and sets up kings; he gives wisdom to the wise and knowledge to those who have understanding; he reveals deep and hidden things; he knows what is in the darkness, and the light dwells with him. To you, O God of my fathers, I give thanks and praise, for you have given me wisdom and might, and have now made known to me what we asked of you, for you have made known to us the king's matter." Therefore Daniel went in to Arioch, whom the king had appointed to destroy the wise men of Babylon. He went and said thus to him, "Do not destroy the wise men of Babylon; bring me in before the king, and I will show the king the interpretation." (Daniel 2:11-24)

"I saw in the visions of my head as I lay in bed, and behold, a watcher, a holy one, came down from heaven. He proclaimed aloud and said thus: 'Chop down the tree and lop off its branches, strip off its leaves and scatter its fruit. Let the beasts flee from under it and the birds from its branches. But leave the stump of its roots in the earth, bound with a band of iron and bronze, amid the tender grass of the field. Let him be wet with the dew of heaven. Let his portion be with the beasts in the grass of the earth. Let his mind be changed from a man's, and let a beast's mind be given to him; and let seven periods of time pass over him. The sentence is by the decree of the watchers, the decision by the word of the holy ones, to the end that the living may know that the Most High rules the kingdom of men and gives it to whom he will and sets over it the lowliest of men.' This dream I, King Nebuchadnezzar, saw. And you, O Belteshazzar, tell me the interpretation, because all the wise men of my kingdom are not able to make known to me the interpretation, but you are able, for the spirit of the holy gods is in you." Then Daniel, whose name was Belteshazzar, was dismayed for a while, and his thoughts alarmed him. The king answered and said, "Belteshazzar, let not the dream or the interpretation alarm you." Belteshazzar answered and said, "My lord, may the dream be for those who hate you and its interpretation for your enemies! The tree you saw, which grew and became strong, so that its top reached to heaven, and it was visible to the end of the whole earth, whose leaves were beautiful and its fruit abundant, and in which was food for all, under which beasts of the field found shade, and in whose branches the birds of the heavens lived—it is you, O king, who have grown and become strong. Your greatness has grown and reaches to heaven, and your dominion to the ends of the earth. And because the king saw a watcher, a holy one, coming down from heaven and saying, 'Chop down the tree and destroy it, but leave the stump of its roots in the earth, bound with a band of iron and bronze, in the tender grass of the field, and let him be wet with the dew of heaven, and let his portion be with the beasts of the field, till seven periods of time pass over him,' this is the interpretation, O king: It is a decree of the Most High, which has come upon my lord the king, that you shall be driven from among men, and your dwelling shall be with the beasts of the field. You shall be made to eat grass like an ox, and you shall be wet with the dew of heaven, and seven periods of time shall pass over you, till you know that the Most High rules the kingdom of men and gives it to whom he will. (Daniel 4:13-25)

Immediately the word was fulfilled against Nebuchadnezzar. He was driven from among men and ate grass like an ox, and his body was wet with the dew of heaven till his hair grew as long as eagles' feathers, and his nails were like birds' claws. At the end of the days I, Nebuchadnezzar, lifted my eyes to heaven, and my reason returned to me, and I blessed the Most High, and praised and honored him who lives forever, for his dominion is an everlasting dominion, and his kingdom endures from generation to generation; all the inhabitants of the earth are accounted as nothing, and he does according to his will among the host of heaven and among the inhabitants of the earth; and none can stay his hand or say to him, "What have you done?" At the same time my reason returned to me, and for the glory of my kingdom, my majesty and splendor returned to me. My counselors and my lords sought me, and I was established in my kingdom, and still more greatness was added to me. Now I, Nebuchadnezzar, praise and extol and honor the King of heaven, for all his works are right and his ways are just; and those who walk in pride he is able to humble. (Daniel 4:33-37)

CARPE DIEM

A few years ago a movie named *The Dead Poet's Society* resurrected an obscure Latin phrase, *carpe diem*. *Carpe diem* means, Seize the day. It means to grab life for all the gusto you can, to take advantage of every opportunity, to live life to the fullest. As a philosophy, *carpe diem* has a strain of the ancient humanistic axiom, I am the captain of my own fate. The only problem with that philosophy is… well, life. Life is bigger than your power to seize it and control it. Ask the people recovering from the latest hurricane what their Palm Pilots looked like the day the hurricane hit. They may have had all kinds of to-do lists for that day. But all plans were put on hold in order to seek cover from an unexpected storm. They did not seize the day. The day seized them.

What do you do when the day seizes you? When life comes to you with a crisis, your destiny is forged in your response to those moments—moments when the telephone rings at 2 a.m., moments when you don't get the promotion you had been working for, moments when you don't get into the graduate school you had planned on, or moments when a perfect retirement plan is interrupted by a lab report. No, in those moments you don't seize life. It seizes you. Where is God's will for your life then?

In Daniel 2 life seized Daniel. But in this chapter God faithfully worked out Daniel's destiny. The crisis of a troubled king's dream and his insane mandate became the catalyst that propelled Daniel into God's plans. Looking into the truths of these Scriptures will give us faith-building divine insight into how God forges our destiny in Him through every situation we face in this life.

God Forges Our Destiny in One Moment—One terrifying moment unleashed the Word of God in one man's life (Daniel 2:1-5, 11-13)

The situation is this: Nebuchadnezzar had a dream. The dream troubled him. In Daniel it seems that this king is always dreaming and his dreams always intersect Daniel's life! This is, of course, the way life is. Your life, for good or bad, your dreams end up touching my life. We do not live in a vacuum. Our hopes and dreams go forward in the mishmash of other dreams. This is where our destiny is forged.

Following Nebuchadnezzar's first dream, the mighty but increasingly disturbed monarch demands that his wise men interpret his dream. The response of the court seers and magicians is pretty much, No problem, King. They had figured out long ago some of the secrets of suggestion and other ways to psychologically manipulate this inflated ego of a man. But this time the king said, "No. You must also tell me what I dreamed!" This threw a monkey wrench into the situation! Moreover, he threatened that if they could not tell him his bad dream, it would be a nightmare for them! The moral may well be, Don't get into the path of a brewing storm or a king who is having trouble sleeping!

The Word of God does what it does so often. The affairs of state, the great national events of history interconnect with the ordinary life of one believer. This is what I love about the Word of God. Today you can trust that God is going to bring His Word to bear on your life. This is not far away history; it is God's Word coming to you. By this time Daniel was part of the court of the wise men. Arioch, the commander of the king's guard, appears before our man Daniel and, with one hand on a giant sword, thrusts the other hand out with a royal decree: Tell me the dream or lose your head.

In Daniel 1, Daniel was faced with a moment of crisis. He would either serve God or apostatize the faith. Now Daniel's experience of God's faithfulness would come down to a single moment in time. Bryan Chapell's fine book *Standing Your Ground* characterizes such moments as the times when the bottom falls out.[2]

The bottom fell out for Ned in one moment. Ned was my boss. His name really should have been Nebuchadnezzar. Ned was the Babylonian king in my life! I was a manager, and he was the manager of managers for Ashland and reported to the very top of our Fortune 500 company. Ned was a product of a tough, Ohio-steel-town, blue-collar, smoke-stack rearing. He had made his way up from there to get a good education, but he never lost his steel-town, blue-collar, tough-guy image. And faith? Well, Ned equated Christianity with weakness. He took particular delight in using the foulest language imaginable in front of believers. He worked hard, and after meetings at night, Ned lived hard. He expected his managers, and I was one of them, to work and live and party like he did. You wouldn't call it persecution, but you would call it workplace intimidation. If I was going to be successful with the company, I had to play his game. I wanted to honor him as my superior, but I couldn't go along with his vulgarity, and particularly, I could not tolerate his using Christ's name in vain. One day I told him so, and he blew up to the point of screaming at me to get away from him before he hit me. I did. I would have been fired long be-

---

[2] Bryan Chapell, *Standing Your Ground: A Call to Courage in an Age of Compromise: Messages from Daniel* (Grand Rapids, Michigan: Baker Book House, 1989), 39.

fore this time except for one thing: our business was doing very well in the Midwest. Well, the only thing I knew to do was to pray for Ned. I prayed and asked others to join me in praying for his salvation. And God saved him. How it happened need not be repeated here, but when it happened, our relationship changed instantly. His nemesis—Yours Truly—became his best friend. Ned flew from Chicago to Kansas City to tell me about his new life in Jesus Christ. I watched as Ned began his journey of faith. Like any baby, he was awkward as he began to walk in this new faith. Still boastful, still rough around the edges, Ned looked like me in many ways, but especially he reminded me of a pre-resurrection Peter: clearly a rough piece of work under construction. But it all came down to one moment. I had committed myself to thirty days of prayer for Ned's sanctification. I had become his best friend. He tried to promote me two times, but by this time I knew I was going to seminary. Ned had figured that as well and even told me so. But one day he called me. The bottom had fallen out. The old Ned had crept into a conversation with a lady at our office in Minneapolis, and he had said the wrong thing. Now a harassment suit was being filed. Ned confessed his mistake to me, and then he said, "Mike, tomorrow the VP of Human Resources is flying down the legal eagles. It's over. Will you come to Chicago and be with me?" I flew out to sit and pray with my boss and my friend. His world as a highflying executive was coming to an end. We talked and we prayed. We prayed a lot. And then we prayed some more until the secretary knocked on the door and said, "They're here." I said goodbye and walked out. I passed the Human Resources guy in the hall. I knew him, and we exchanged muted greeting. I looked back and could see into Ned's office. There was a new Christian. The bottom had dropped out. The world had come apart for Ned. In that moment, he would live out his destiny as a new believer. I wondered, Did my prayers for His sanctification bring this on? I don't know about that, but when Ned's old world fell apart, God's creative power began to work in his life.

Has anyone here ever had his or her world fall apart? Has anyone here ever had the bottom drop out? Maybe you had a situation like Ned? Or maybe it was different for you. Maybe it was a dreaded telephone ringing in the middle of the night, and you wake to ask, "Where is my teen?" Maybe it was a moment frozen in time when your wife said, "I'm leaving you." Maybe it was a pain in your chest. Maybe your dreams just keep getting battered, one storm after another, and it doesn't seem to ever stop.

My beloved, God is not absent in such moments. Your faith, a faith which was given to you by Christ, will not fail. In fact, the book of Daniel is here to say that when your world falls apart, God's wall of protection will become the only thing you have.

Such frozen moments have to yield to a decision, a response. Those next moments can change your life.

God Can Forge the Destiny of Many Lives through One Life—One consecrated life influenced the whole of history (Daniel 2:14-16)

In Daniel 2:14-16, the moment of terror becomes a moment of decision for Daniel. He inquires of Arioch,"Why did the king issue such a harsh decree?" We are not given the answer to that question. But Arioch, we are told, explains the matter to Daniel.

> At this, Daniel went into the king and asked for time, so that he might interpret the dream for him (Daniel 2:16, NIV).

In our language, some hot shot was throwing the meanest fastball ever thrown and said this thing is coming at you. And Daniel steps up to the plate.

One life. One consecrated life. Can it make a difference?

I refer you again to a main point I find in this book and other books in the Bible. The main point is that history is not just what historians call a higher history, made up simply of empires and kings and queens. History is written through the extraordinary faith of ordinary everyday people in extraordinary day-to-day living. Life is not just about impersonal nation-states and successful or failed military strategies; life is about…well…lives and how we live them.

A good example of this is seen in the flow from the Judges to Ruth to 1 Samuel. The book of Judges ends with the statement that all of Israel did what was right in their own eyes. The reader is left to say, Well, this thing is a bust. The nation is unfaithful; therefore, God's plans will fail. But then we are led to the book Ruth. There we see how one godly widow, a pagan who cast her lot with God's people rather than return to her pagan nation, became a woman of faith who married her redeemer, Boaz. From that marriage a great line of faith would continue. The nation is still corrupt, but God is at work in the unseen but very normal things of life. Then we move to 1 Samuel, and the first person we encounter is a faithful lass named Hannah. Hannah's faith in the midst of her personal struggles and hardships becomes a clue for the believer. God's plans are not dependent on great nations but on the faithful lives of individual believers, in these cases the lives of faithful women of God. One consecrated life can influence all of history. In this case, Hannah's faith leads to Hannah's miracle, Samuel, who leads a people to God's greater blessing because Samuel anoints David. The son of Hannah anoints the King of Israel, who is the great grandson of Ruth. It is amazing. One life makes a difference. And so it goes through the Bible until we get to one faithful carpenter named Joseph and the miracle of one little lass from Nazareth named Mary. One life.

Someone had to reach the center of Africa, and David Livingston said, I am that man. One Christian had to bring Christ and humanity to the destitute in India, and Amy Carmichael said, I am that person. This week a Ugandan pastor was in my office, a friend who heard the question, Who will plant a church in a Moslem controlled area next to the capital of Uganda; and he said, I am that man.

Beloved, who will be the next missionaries to the ends of the earth? One life right here who says, I am that woman. Who will pastor our people and plant new churches in our nation? Someone here must say, I am that man. Who will be the Christian to show compassion and love to the loveless, to the unlovable in our community? One person here must say, I will. Who will be the prayer warrior for our nation in need of revival? One life can make a difference, so I must. Who will leave this world and receive Jesus Christ as Lord?

The truth of this passage and the whole Word of God is that your life makes a difference in this world. Entire histories are written on one life consecrated to Jesus Christ.

God Can Change a Person's Destiny through One Prayer—One fervent prayer changed the course of the world (Daniel 2:17-18)

Daniel immediately responded to this traumatic event by alerting his friends to pray.

> He urged them to plead for mercy from the God of heaven concerning this mystery, so that he and his friends might not be executed with the rest of the wise men (Daniel 2:18, NIV).

Brothers and sisters, our destiny is forged in prayer.

> The effectual fervent prayer of a righteous man availeth much.
> (James 5:16, KJV).

Daniel's life and destiny was changed through prayer. God calls us to look to Him in the traumas of our lives, and He will be there.

As a pastor, I am amazed at how prayer changes the lives of the people I see. In fact, it is fascinating. And seeing your faith strengthens my own faith. Yesterday I talked to a Major Roberts who lives in South Alabama. He told me what life was like as he had to go through Hurricane Ivan. He said that he and his wife and three teenagers knelt down and prayed and asked God to spare them. He said, "Children, we can trust God no matter what happens. Let us pray that God will spare us, but let us remember that though a thousand fall at our left hand and ten thousand at our right, He will take care of us—in life or in death. We are God's people!" I was amazed at his faith. He told me, "Chaplain, we were eating pancakes and bacon and watching Country Music TV the next morning! The electricity didn't even go out!" It was his way of saying that God was good. Then he said, "Chaplain, those kids will never forget how God answered prayer." We admitted that it is a mystery why he was spared and others experienced loss. But there is no mystery in going to God in prayer; we are always changed when we come into the presence of God.

Later yesterday, I listened to how a crisis drove another family to prayer. I stood with a family from our community over the hospital bed of their loved one at the University of Alabama Trauma Center. This young man has a critical brain injury, the victim of a crime, and is in a drug-induced coma. With his mother, brother, sister-in-law, and girlfriend, we gathered around the young man's bed. I listened to them tell about God's love and faithfulness in their own storm of life. As I left, the family said, "Thank you for your prayers. We are being blessed by them. And please pray for him." They trusted that out of this crisis, God would be there.

Two families, two very different kinds of storms, but like Daniel, their response is the same: Take it to the Lord in prayer.

This is where God meets you, my beloved, in good times and bad. It is as if all of these things happen, forging our destiny to be close to Him until we finally see Him face-to-face. Then we will look back on how He was always there with us in prayer.

God Transforms the Destiny of His Enemies through One Testimony—One faithful testimony led the hardest case to turn to God (Daniel 2:19-24; 4:13-25, 33-37)

The dream revelation and interpretation is at the very core of what this story is about. As I said in my last message on Daniel, you can take a prophetic approach in this book and spend time studying the beauty and accuracy of the dreams and visions, which is glorious. But my concern here is to look at what God teaches us about discipleship. Here we see that Daniel's prayerful response to the crisis leads him to reveal the dreams to Nebuchadnezzar.

First, he reveals the dream at hand. There is an image with a head of gold, which represents Nebuchadnezzar's kingdom. But that will not last forever. Another will follow. The image had a chest and arms of a less expensive mineral, silver. That represents a lesser power, the Medes and Persians. Then there will be a third power of bronze. In history we can identify this power as the Greeks, who did in fact follow the Persian Empire. Then, finally the image had legs of iron and feet made of iron and clay. This is the fourth kingdom. This kingdom will be struck on the feet by a rock, and when it falls, all the image will fall. That rock represents the Lord Jesus Christ. His kingdom is more powerful than all the other kingdoms put together. And that rock, which was not cut with human hands, represents an out-of-this-world kingdom. Thus, with His coming, Jesus would say, "The kingdom of God is at hand." This is what Jesus came preaching. And we read in Revelation,

> "The kingdom of the world has become the kingdom of our Lord and of his Christ, and he will reign for ever and ever" (Revelation 11:15).

Christ's kingdom is a kingdom that is like leaven in a bowl of dough, working its way through all the rest.[3] It is a kingdom that is like a mustard seed,[4] starting small but growing to produce a giant tree where birds could nest. His kingdom is here. This fifth monarchy is the most powerful kingdom in history and is the only permanent kingdom. As Nebuchadnezzar was being shown that his kingdom will not last forever, you need to remember that your life will not last forever. You need to place your trust in Jesus Christ. Christians need to remember whose subjects they are and line up their lives with Christ at the top.

---

[3] He told them still another parable: "The kingdom of heaven is like yeast that a woman took and mixed into a large amount of flour until it worked all through the dough" (Matthew 13:33, NIV).

[4] He told them another parable: "The kingdom of heaven is like a mustard seed, which a man took and planted in his field" (Matthew 13:31, NIV).

The second dream, which occurs in Daniel 4, is related by Nebuchadnezzar himself and, again, is interpreted by Daniel. The dream is of a tree that is large and beautiful. It represents the kingdom of Nebuchadnezzar. But a holy one comes down and makes a declaration that the tree must come down. This, Daniel says, is the decree of God to show that Nebuchadnezzar has grown proud in the face of God. He did not give glory to God. A stump is left showing that God would restore him after "seven periods of time" pass over him, indicating the fullness of God's timetable. During this time, Nebuchadnezzar would go out into the field and eat grass like an ox and live outside like an animal. All of this is to show that "…the Most High rules the kingdom of men and gives it to whom he will" (Daniel 4:32).

Nebuchadnezzar himself tells us that this is exactly what happened. His unbelief led him to madness; but after a season, he recovered his senses, literally, and regained his throne. By then, Nebuchadnezzar was a changed man who closed out Daniel 4 with a song of praise that begins,

> "for his dominion is an everlasting dominion, and his kingdom endures from generation to generation…" (Daniel 4:34).

All unbelief robs us of our true humanity. It always leads to the debasing of life. Only faith in Jesus Christ can lift up our head from the bestial condition of our sins and give us new life.

All of this ministry came from one faithful testimony that led to the hardest case turning to God. You see, God put Daniel in Babylon to reach the greatest pagan empire on earth. God's heart was set on being glorified by the treacherous and diabolical emperor of Babylon being converted to bring praise to the King of kings and the Lord of lords.

This past week I read in *World Magazine* about a young Army captain who answered the question, Why are you in Iraq? He sees himself there to not only flush out the enemies of freedom, but to find the captives of sin and ignorance and share Jesus' love with little children and with Islamic peoples. He sees his destiny as an ambassador of Christ to Iraq for such a time as this. A crises of war has led to a testimony of grace.

That is what happened in Daniel's life, and that is what happens in our lives as we say, "Lord use me, right where I am, right here in this unexpected place in my life."

Conclusion

Time and time again I heard about how people who were leaving their homes as the hurricanes came at them were told to forget everything and just leave. But you all know what they took, don't you? That's right. They took photos. I know what they mean. The other night I stopped in our hall and looked at the photos on the wall there. As I looked at the photo of Aunt Eva, I was drawn to see something more than photographic paper matted and framed. I saw how God's love placed me in the care of a woman who prayed for me all of my life. When I looked at the photo of my father as a young naval lieutenant, I did not just see that young man; but I was drawn to see the God who would lead him through all of his sin to see the grace and love he had always wanted and would one day discover. We are drawn to our photos because there is another story behind them.

The book of Daniel draws me, not just to an Old Testament hero, but the more I read Daniel, the more I see the image of One in Gethsemane praying to His Father to keep those whom He had chosen. Daniel draws us to Calvary where the destiny of God's people literally hung on a cross. Daniel draws us to the tomb where the body of Jesus lay. And it draws us to imagine the power of God flowing through Jesus and raising Him up—the first fruits among many brethren. And that is where our Jesus lives—in the storms, the crimes, where the edict of the enemy comes face-to-face with the promises of our God. That is where God meets us and calls us to follow Him and realize our destiny—not in seizing the day, but in surrendering to the grace of a loving Savior.

Questions for Reflection

1. Think of a time when you felt "the bottom fall out" of your life. How did God use that to strengthen your faith in His presence and sovereign power?

2. In Daniel, we learn that history is not just written by kings and wars and treaties, but by individuals. Who did God use in your own history to influence the disciple of Jesus you are today? How were they used? How did God use difficult people in your life to strengthen you to do His will?

3. How has your prayer life been enriched through trial? Do you think that it is possible to cultivate a life of devout and earnest prayer without the presence of difficulties? Think through how blessings can work toward enriching our prayer life.

4. Has God ever placed you in a situation where your life could be used to influence an unbeliever? Reflect on that. How did it go? What if that happened today? What things would you do differently if the Lord placed you as His ambassador in the presence of an unbeliever?

Prayer

Father of grace, by whose Spirit You moved across the face of the deep to bring about a new world and by whose Spirit You now move across the lives of the lost to bring the Good News of Jesus, use me. Use me, Lord, as you please. Help me to be ready when You do. In Christ's precious name.

Amen.

"God calls some to win by living. Others are called to win by dying. But in life or death God rules and we are called to serve Him."

James Montgomery Boice

"When through fiery trials thy pathway shall lie,
My grace, all sufficient, shall be thy supply;
The flame shall not hurt thee; I only design
Thy dross to consume, and thy gold to refine."

John Rippon

3

FACING THE FIRE AND LIVING WITH LIONS

Daniel 3:8-12, 16-26; 6:3-10, 14-24

Today we come to one of the most famous parts of the Book of Daniel: the fiery trials of three boys who would not bow down to the golden image of Nebuchadnezzar and the lion's den that made Daniel so famous.

In these familiar stories of faith, God gives not just great heroes but a living hope.

> Therefore at that time certain Chaldeans came forward and maliciously accused the Jews. They declared to King Nebuchadnezzar, "O king, live forever! You, O king, have made a decree, that every man who hears the sound of the horn, pipe, lyre, trigon, harp, bagpipe, and every kind of music, shall fall down and worship the golden image. And whoever does not fall down and worship shall be cast into a burning fiery furnace. There are certain Jews whom you have appointed over the affairs of the province of Babylon: Shadrach, Meshach, and Abednego. These men, O king, pay no attention to you; they do not serve your gods or worship the golden image that you have set up." (Daniel 3:8-12)
>
> Shadrach, Meshach, and Abednego answered and said to the king, "O Nebuchadnezzar, we have no need to answer you in this matter. If this be so, our God whom we serve is able to deliver us from the burning fiery furnace, and he will deliver us out of your hand, O king. But if not, be it known to you, O king, that we will not serve your gods or worship the golden image that you have set up." Then Nebuchadnezzar was filled with fury, and the expression of his face was changed against Shadrach, Meshach, and Abednego. He ordered the furnace heated seven times more than it was usually heated. And he ordered some of the mighty men of his army to bind Shadrach, Meshach, and Abednego, and to cast them into the burning fiery furnace. Then these men were bound in their

cloaks, their tunics, their hats, and their other garments, and they were thrown into the burning fiery furnace. Because the king's order was urgent and the furnace overheated, the flame of the fire killed those men who took up Shadrach, Meshach, and Abednego. And these three men, Shadrach, Meshach, and Abednego, fell bound into the burning fiery furnace. Then King Nebuchadnezzar was astonished and rose up in haste. He declared to his counselors, "Did we not cast three men bound into the fire?" They answered and said to the king, "True, O king." He answered and said, "But I see four men unbound, walking in the midst of the fire, and they are not hurt; and the appearance of the fourth is like a son of the gods." Then Nebuchadnezzar came near to the door of the burning fiery furnace; he declared, "Shadrach, Meshach, and Abednego, servants of the Most High God, come out, and come here!" Then Shadrach, Meshach, and Abednego came out from the fire. (Daniel 3:16-26)

Then this Daniel became distinguished above all the other presidents and satraps, because an excellent spirit was in him. And the king planned to set him over the whole kingdom. Then the presidents and the satraps sought to find a ground for complaint against Daniel with regard to the kingdom, but they could find no ground for complaint or any fault, because he was faithful, and no error or fault was found in him. Then these men said, "We shall not find any ground for complaint against this Daniel unless we find it in connection with the law of his God." Then these presidents and satraps came by agreement to the king and said to him, "O King Darius, live forever! All the presidents of the kingdom, the prefects and the satraps, the counselors and the governors are agreed that the king should establish an ordinance and enforce an injunction, that whoever makes petition to any god or man for thirty days, except to you, O king, shall be cast into the den of lions. Now, O king, establish the injunction and sign the document, so that it cannot be changed, according to the law of the Medes and the Persians, which cannot be revoked." Therefore King Darius signed the document and injunction. When Daniel knew that the document had been signed, he went to his house where he had windows in his upper chamber open toward Jerusalem. He got down on his knees three times a day and prayed and gave thanks before his God, as he had done previously. (Daniel 6:3-10)

Then the king, when he heard these words, was much distressed and set his mind to deliver Daniel. And he labored till the sun went down to rescue him. Then these men came by agreement to the king and said to the king, "Know, O king, that it is a law of the Medes and Persians that no injunction or ordinance that the king establishes can be changed." Then the king commanded, and Daniel was brought and cast into the den of lions. The king declared to Daniel, "May your

God, whom you serve continually, deliver you!" And a stone was brought and laid on the mouth of the den, and the king sealed it with his own signet and with the signet of his lords, that nothing might be changed concerning Daniel. Then the king went to his palace and spent the night fasting; no diversions were brought to him, and sleep fled from him. Then, at break of day, the king arose and went in haste to the den of lions. As he came near to the den where Daniel was, he cried out in a tone of anguish. The king declared to Daniel, "O Daniel, servant of the living God, has your God, whom you serve continually, been able to deliver you from the lions?" Then Daniel said to the king, "O king, live forever! My God sent his angel and shut the lions' mouths, and they have not harmed me, because I was found blameless before him; and also before you, O king, I have done no harm." Then the king was exceedingly glad, and commanded that Daniel be taken up out of the den. So Daniel was taken up out of the den, and no kind of harm was found on him, because he had trusted in his God. And the king commanded, and those men who had maliciously accused Daniel were brought and cast into the den of lions—they, their children, and their wives. And before they reached the bottom of the den, the lions overpowered them and broke all their bones in pieces. (Daniel 6:14-24)

THE MYSTERY OF FAITH

The great G.K. Chesterton wrote in his wonderful book *Orthodoxy*, that "As long as you have mystery you have health."[1] Is that true? Is that biblically orthodox?

Is true faith knowing precisely which way to go? Or is true faith taking the hand of God and walking forward though you really have no idea where you will end up?

We have moved through a time in North American Christianity when we seemed to have wrapped faith up in a nice package with a bow on it. In the most bizarre and plainly unbiblical forms, faith is equated with health and wealth. This, of course, flies in the face off a suffering Savior who had no place to lay his head. But in more mainstream Christianity, sermons are said to be effective when they are relevant. Usually that works out as "Seven Ways to Avoid Burnout in Your Life" or "Nine Ways to Make Sure Your Kids Turn Out OK." There is nothing wrong with "How To" sermons. But there is a problem with using the Bible as a way to make God fit into a box or reduce the mysteries of life to "how to" points that resolve all problems with just a few be-

[1] http://www.ccel.org/c/chesterton/orthodoxy/ch2.html

havioral modifications. The problem with such sermons, like the problem with a snake-oil salesman advertising a happy marriage for whoever buys his love potion number 9, is that life doesn't always conform to philosophical syllogisms or nine-point happy-life sermons or potions. Our faith is best lived out in mystery. So I think Chesterton was right.

By mystery, I do not mean (nor did Chesterton) that we can't know God or His Word. We most certainly can and must. But the faith that comes and is built up in that Word is lived out in the unpredictable, transient, paradoxical places called life. It is a place where the beauty of nature, say a magnificent mountain, becomes a merciless killer to a mountain climber. It is a place, kids, where, if you cheat on your examine, you are expelled, but if a newsman does it, he is on the air again the next night. It is a place where innocent people are murdered by brutal terrorists, and yet, it is a place where God lives and where, in the midst of it all, we are promised peace by the One who is called the Prince of Peace. Admitting that mystery, as Chesterton suggests, leads to a health (and I would say a spiritual health).

We could put it like this: I don't know the future, but I know the One who holds the future. Faith in uncertainty, or as a former assistant pastor of mine would learn to put it, I do not know why the accident happened that took the life of my brother, but I know that God is there.

This is a faith that trusts in a God who is there in fiery furnaces and lion's dens.

As we turn to Daniel 3 and 6, we will come face-to-face with God's picture of true faith. The attitudes of biblical faithfulness seen in the three men in the furnace and in Daniel in the lion's den lead us to discover four facets of true faith that will give us the spiritual strength to stand in the mysteries of our lives.

True Faith Is Established, Not Just in the Encouragement of Friends, but in the Accusations of the Enemy (Daniel 3:8-12; 6:3-9)

In the first case, the three Hebrews (Shadrach, Meshach, and Abednego) are targeted by certain Chaldeans who accuse them of not bowing down. There is a plot to destroy these men. Later, when Babylon is under the control of the Medes and Persians and Darius is king, an identical thing happens to Daniel. There are those who are jealous of Daniel, who has become a governor and is well on his way to becoming the prime minister of the whole kingdom (Daniel 6:3). They looked for a way to trip him but none was found. So in Daniel 6:5, they figure that the only way to get him is through his faith in the one true God. Thus, the plot begins. They conspire to establish an ordinance and to get an injunction that anyone who prays to any god or man except to Darius for thirty days will be thrown into a den of lions. The king signs it, and it seems the enemy has gotten rid of Daniel.

Names change but the plot stays the same. This is what happened with the plot against Joseph in the case of Potipher's wife. In Esther a jealous and maniacal underling named Hamaan plots to kill all the Jews. And on and on it goes. Until at last we read of how the unbelieving Jewish religious leaders conspire to undo the Savior:

The Pharisees went out and immediately held counsel with the Herodians against him, how to destroy him (Mark 3:6). Judas, too, becomes one who conspires with them, out of his own evil heart, to destroy Jesus.

The same motif continues in the New Testament records as we see how Paul spoke about the plots of the Jews (Acts 20:19). The book of Revelation teaches us that after the dragon, representing Satan, could not destroy the child of the woman, speaking of Jesus, this serpent went after Jesus' people.

Psalm 2 speaks to this when it says,

> Why do the nations rage
> and the peoples plot in vain?
> The kings of the earth set themselves,
> and the rulers take counsel together,
> against the LORD and against his anointed, saying,
> "Let us burst their bonds apart
> and cast away their cords from us."

Jesus identified those who opposed Him and sought to kill Him when He said,

> "You are of your father the devil, and your will is to do your father's desires. He was a murderer from the beginning, and has nothing to do with the truth, because there is no truth in him. When he lies, he speaks out of his own character, for he is a liar and the father of lies" (John 8:44).

The Bible is teaching that faith does not exist in a vacuum. Real spiritual warfare is going on in the lives of believers. Being a Christian is not tiptoeing through the tulips of life. It is life lived in the presence of the enemy. The Bible teaches us several things about this.

- Those who are Christ's people and who live for Christ can anticipate that their faith will be targeted for attack. Jesus told us that the servant is no greater than the Master.
- Those who do such things, unwittingly or not, are playing into the hand of the enemy. This is why, in John 8:44, Jesus told those Jewish leaders who opposed Him, "You are of your father the devil."
- Because Jesus was and remains victorious, everything that comes against you, comes against Jesus and, therefore, cannot be ultimately victorious. Eleven of the twelve apostles went to be with the Lord because of martyrdom. Our own times have witnessed unspeakable atrocities against Christians because of true faith. But I say that there will be ultimate victory because God says so. Paul speaks a litany of crimes against Christians, and then says that we are more than conquers through these very things because of Christ who loves us. The book of Revelation speaks of martyrs gathered under the very throne of Christ. They cry out for vindication, and it shall come in the judgment of a Savior who stands for His people.

So, where does that leave us? It leaves us where it left Shadrach, Meshach, and Abednego, and where it left Daniel. Our faith does not depend upon good times. Our faith is actually strengthened in such times. In church history, faith has even come in such times.

I have mentioned before about a time when I stood in a great amphitheatre that had been unearthed in Durrës, Albania. As I toured the facility, I was shown cages which had held the wild animals used to eat Christians. But I noticed that in these cells were beautiful mosaics embedded into the walls. When I inquired about them, I was told that these cells, which once had held the wild beasts that were unleashed to destroy believers, became the very thing that unleashed true revival in the Roman provinces. And the very cages which had held animals to destroy the faith of Christ's people were transformed into chapels to worship Christ and build up the faith of Christ's people.

Beloved, don't fret over the presence of accusers. What God did for Joseph, for the three Hebrew children, for Daniel, for Esther and Mordecai and the Jews of that day, for Paul and for Peter, He will do for you. For if you have trusted Jesus, you now have the King of kings and Lord of lords as your defense. He has taken on accusers, and through the paradox of the cross where the enemy thought he had won, Christ became the victor once and for all. Thus,

> A thousand may fall at your side,
> ten thousand at your right hand,
> but [the enemy] will not come near you (Psalms 91:7).

True Faith Is Confirmed, Not in the Fiery Furnace or in the Lion's Den, but in the Decisions That Bring Us There (Daniel 3:16)

The Lord has blessed us with numerous lawyers in our midst. And, yes, I said blessed! Just try being accused of something in a court and not having a lawyer with you! Or think of the prosecutors who also stand up for us! Or the judges who ensure that our constitutional rights are preserved in the judicial system. I am told that much goes on between the defense and the prosecution before the trial ever begins. There are pre-trial motions and negotiations between attorneys and so forth. And that is certainly true in matters of our faith. Before the actual trial begins, there are pre-trial motions. In fact, for the believer, it is because of his decision to follow God that he even ends up in the fires or in the lion's dens of life!

Shadrach, Meshach and Abednego simply could not bow to another god. And Daniel could not yield to the edict not to pray to the Lord. Peter was told not to preach Christ, but he said, "We must obey God rather than man."[2] Paul was repeatedly beaten for preaching Christ, but what choice did he have as a follower of Christ?

True faith did not happen for the three Hebrews in the fiery furnace. That was when God came and stood beside them. True faith did not happen for Daniel in the lion's den for it was God's part to stop the mouths of the lions He had made. It was not Peter's faith that released him from prison, but the power of God. And my beloved, the great faith that we are called to return to the Lord is not at the moment of the crisis, but in that moment when a decision is made to follow God.

During the Reformation in England, the Archbishop of Canterbury, Thomas Cranmer, was also the man who was primarily responsible for the soundly scriptural and beautiful *Book of Common Prayer*. When Thomas Cranmer was called to stand for the gospel of grace, which was at the core of biblical faith as held by those Reformers, Bloody Mary threatened him with the stake! But he did what the Hebrew children who faced the fire did. He did what Daniel who faced the lion's den did. He did what Peter did and Paul did and so many before him did.

What would you do if you were told to recant your faith in the gospel of grace? Would you stand, though you look through the bars of your cell to see the servants

---

[2] And when they had brought them, they set them before the council. And the high priest questioned them, saying, "We strictly charged you not to teach in this name, yet here you have filled Jerusalem with your teaching, and you intend to bring this man's blood upon us." But Peter and the apostles answered, "We must obey God rather than men" (Acts 5:27-29).

carrying the wood to the stake to be prepared for your execution by burning? Well, Cranmer made the decision to stand for Christ, but then he gave in. In fact, the mad Queen, the daughter of Cathrine of Aragon who had been wrongly divorced and ousted from London by Henry VIII in favor of a new woman and a new sort of Christianity, wanted nothing more than for this Reformed church leader to recant his views and be seen as a coward. So dangling between the judgment of being burned for faith in the gospel of grace or being freed for a religion of works, he recanted his confession! All of Reformed England bowed her head in shame. But then Bloody Mary said, "Ah ha! I appreciate your recantation **but you will burn anyway!**" And so the fires were lit again. And in the solitary place of a cell, Cranmer realized that his only freedom, his only safety, was in the eternal arms of God, not in the whims of a troubled woman; and he recanted his recantation! As he was led to his death, he asked that the hand that had originally signed his recantation of grace be placed so that it would be the first to burn. Though he was fearful and though he retreated from his stand for Christ, in the end the power of God that gave him saving faith, gave him faith to stand. And as he forgave his executioner and the queen herself, revival began to sweep England.

I have been told by mature believers, "I don't think I could stand for Christ in times of affliction." My beloved, do not worry about the fire. Do not worry about the lion's den. When the hour of decision comes to you, the One who called you to that hour will not forsake you. The very words, the very decision, the very act of courage is found, not in yourself, but in the Spirit of Jesus Christ inside of you.

True Faith Is Dependent, Not on Knowing the Mystery of God's Decretive Will, but in Knowing the Certainty of God's Revealed Will (Daniel 3:17-18; 6:10)

Now before I unpack that, let me tell where I coming from. In Daniel 3:17-18 we have the record of the three Hebrew boys:

> "If we are thrown into the blazing furnace, the God we serve is able to save us from it, and he will rescue us from your hand, O king. But even if he does not, we want you to know, O king, that we will not serve your gods or worship the image of gold you have set up" (Daniel 3:17-18, NIV).

In Daniel 6:10 we have the response of Daniel:

> Now when Daniel learned that the decree had been published, he went home to his upstairs room where the windows opened toward Jerusa-

lem. Three times a day he got down on his knees and prayed, giving thanks to his God, just as he had done before (Daniel 6:10, NIV).

In both cases, the faith of these young men was not tied to whether or not God would get them out of the bind! Their faith was in the God who had already saved them! The book of Hebrews teaches us that this is true faith.

> Now faith is the assurance of things hoped for, the conviction of things not seen (Hebrews 11:1).

God began his commandments by saying, "I am the LORD your God, who brought you out of the land of Egypt, out of the house of slavery."[3] God is the Savior. There would come a Savior, God's Son, and in Jesus came the fulfillment of all other saving events in redemptive history. And when Jesus was crucified on the cross, He cried, "It is finished!"[4] That is what Daniel and these boys were counting on. They would pray. They would seek God. Even King Darius fasted for Daniel. He wanted Daniel to be saved. But by the time the fires in the furnace were lit so hot that it killed the men who threw them in, the three boys were trusting in God's Word. By the time Daniel was thrown into the lion's den, he was trusting in God's Word. This is the key: these men were not seeking God's unknown will, His decretive will, His will made known to Himself in what He has decreed to happen; but they were trusting in the revealed Word of the Lord. God is a Savior, and they looked to Him alone for their salvation.

The Bible says that we have a word made more sure.[5] The Bible says that in times past God spoke through the prophets, but now He has spoken through His Son.[6] If Shadrach, Meshach, Abednego, and Daniel could trust in the revealed Word of God, we are told that we are in a much better position. They longed to see what we now have:[7] the Son of God revealed to us on earth and His authoritative Word, the Bible, in our possession.

Now I return to this matter of trusting God's will. We do not—nay, we cannot—know what God has decreed and hope to line up our lives to that. Yet

---

[3] Exodus 20:2
[4] John 19:30
[5] And we have something more sure, the prophetic word, to which you will do well to pay attention as to a lamp shining in a dark place, until the day dawns and the morning star rises in your hearts (2 Peter 1:19).
[6] Long ago, at many times and in many ways, God spoke to our fathers by the prophets, but in these last days he has spoken to us by his Son, whom he appointed the heir of all things, through whom also he created the world (Hebrews 1:1).
[7] Concerning this salvation, the prophets who prophesied about the grace that was to be yours searched and inquired carefully (1 Peter 1:10).

that is what Christians mistakenly think of when they think of God's will. But like our examples from Daniel, we turn to God's revealed will in His Word, turn to God in prayer, listen for the Spirit sealing the Word to our hearts, learn to read His providential leading, and follow Him there. But it all begins and ends with God's revealed Word, the Bible.

Now all this is leading us to say that, as in Daniel, we may not know where a decision will take us. It may take us to being saved from that which is seeking to destroy us. Or it may lead us to Jesus face-to-face. Faith does not know the temporal outcome, it does not force God into a position by a magical incantation, but it leans solely on Him through it all and believes that by following Him, we will arrive, eternally, at the best place.

True Faith Is Confirmed by the Presence of Jesus Christ (Daniel 3:24-25; 6:22)

This is a favorite passage of believers because there in the fire we have the testimony of Nebuchadnezzar.

> "Did we not cast three men bound into the fire?...But I see four men unbound, walking in the midst of the fire, and they are not hurt; and the appearance of the fourth is like a son of the gods" (Daniel 3:24-25).

A pagan saw what we know: The Son of God, our Lord Jesus in His pre-incarnate presence, was with those boys.

Who is this fourth man in the fire? He is the One who is in every book of this Bible

> In Genesis—He is the seed of the woman
> In Exodus—He is the Passover Lamb
> In Leviticus—He is our High Priest
> In Numbers—He in the Pillar of Cloud by day and the Pillar of Fire by night
> In Deuteronomy—He is the Prophet like unto Moses
> In Joshua—He is the Captain of our Salvation
> In Judges—He is our Judge and Lawgiver
> In Ruth—He is our Kinsman Redeemer
> In Samuel—He is our Trusted Prophet
> In Kings & Chronicles—He is our Reigning King
> In Ezra—He is our Faithful Scribe
> In Nehemiah—He is the Rebuilder of the broken down walls
> In Esther—He is our Mordecai
> In Job—He is our Ever-Living Redeemer
> In Psalms—He is our Shepherd

> In Proverbs and Ecclesiastes—He is our Wisdom
> In Song of Soloman—He is our Lover and Bridegroom
> In Isaiah—He is the Prince of Peace
> In Jeremiah—He is the Righteous Branch
> In Lamentations—He is the Weeping Prophet
> In Ezekiel—He is the Watchmen over His people
> In Daniel—He is the Fourth Man in the Fire
> In Hosea—He is the Faithful Husband
> In Joel—He is the Baptiser with the Holy Spirit
> In Amos—He is our Burden-Bearer
> In Obadiah—He is Mighty to Save
> In Jonah—He is the Hesed—the grace of God—that reaches the hardest cases
> In Micah—He is the Messenger with Beautiful Feet bringing a message of salvation
> In Nahum—He is the Avenger of God's Elect
> In Habakkuk—He is God's Evangelist
> In Zephaniah—He is our Savior
> In Haggai—He is the Restorer of God's Lost Heritage
> In Zechariah—He is the Fountain open in the House of David to cleanse all sin
> In Malachi—He is the Sun of Righteousness with Healing in His Wing."

Let us say it clearly: The fourth man in the fire, the One who was with Daniel in the lion's den is the One who is the author and finisher of our salvation, the subject of God's revelation to man—that One is the One who is now and forever with every soul who calls on His name. He is Jesus of Nazareth, the Son of God, the righteous One, the promised One, the crucified One, the risen One who said,"I am with you." Who said, "I am the Good shepherd." Who said, "I will never leave you nor forsake you."

As Jesus stood in the fire with those three boys, as he was there with Daniel, He is always there with His people.

Jesus was the fourth man in the fire when James was thrown down from the temple and killed for his faith. Jesus was the fourth man in the fire when Martin Luther stood before his accusers and gave Luther to spirit to say, "Here I stand." Jesus was the fourth man in the fire of my godly Albanian professor who would not bend the knee to Stalin's regime, who was thrown into five years of hard labor for his faith, whose wife was stolen from him for thirty years before they were reunited.

And Jesus is the fourth man in the fire that I see everyday in the lives of people in Chattanooga, Tennessee. Jesus is the fourth man there gathered around loved ones who are going home to be with the Lord. Jesus is the fourth man with believers being wheeled into surgery. He is the fourth man with the Christian surgeon who prays silently, "Lord, give me wisdom; Lord, guide my hands for Your sake…" Jesus is the fourth man with our teachers when they need wisdom to help a failing student. Jesus is the fourth man with our attorneys as they prepare a case for trial. He is the fourth man at the funeral, in marriage counseling. He is the fourth man with you children when you feel like you have no other friends. Jesus is your friend, my child. And He stands with anyone in any situation, no matter where you have been and what you have done, when you say, "Lord Jesus, deliver me. I cast myself completely on your grace and mercy."

For you see, there was no fourth man on the cross. There was no help. He took the hell. He took on the lions. In surrendering to the powers of evil, He rose again and defeated the powers of evil. And He will stand with you.

Will you today, by faith, stand with Him?

Conclusion

Today, I want to sing a song I wrote which was inspired by the study of Daniel and by the fourth man in the fire that I see everyday in your lives. I offer it as an invitation to receive the One who is always there.

> He was there in Babylon
> He was there with Daniel all along
> He was there in the captive's song
> He was there to right the wrong
>
> He was there in the writing on the wall
> He was there in a nation's rise and fall
> He was there guiding the great and small
> He was there and He ordained it all
>
> (Refrain)
> And He was there in the fire
> He was there in the Lion's den
> He was there working all things together
> For good to those who love Him
> And are called by Him
> And that gives me hope
> For my life
> For he is there in my sorrow

He is there in my physical pain
He is there in the sunshine of life
And He's there in the seasons of rain
He is there

He is there when I see Him
He is there when I cannot see HimHe is there when I need Him
He is there when I ignore Him

He was there He is the Ancient of Days
He was there, He's worthy of endless praise
He was there in Daniel's days
He is there in our lives in so many ways

Questions for Reflection

1. What do you think of Chesterton's quote: "As long as you have mystery you have health?" How does that relate to biblically grounded faith?

2. Shadrach, Meshach, and Abednego are targeted by certain Chaldeans who accuse them of not bowing down to the idolatrous image. How does this relate to what you are going through today? Times are different, but if the devices of the Evil One are unchanged, what is the idol? Who is giving the command to bow down? And how are you doing?

3. How is God transforming lion's dens into places of worship in your life? In the lives of believers in our generation?

4. Was the difference between God's "decretive will" and His "revealed will" made plain to you? How could a person possibly err in his or her decision-making by failing to grasp the difference between these two aspects of God's will?

5. Jesus Christ was the "fourth man in the fire" with the Hebrew boys. Jesus Christ is present in all of the Bible as the often unseen but very present Person who is protecting, guiding, and overruling in order to bring blessing to His people and to the world. How has He been the "fourth man in the fire" in your life recently?

Prayer

Lord God, Heavenly Father, by whose strong arm the Hebrews were faithfully protected, I ask you to give me eyes of faith to see You at work in my life. I want to praise the Fourth Man in the Fire. I want to testify to Your presence. I want to open my life to Your presence and power in new ways. Let Your kingdom come in my world. In Jesus' name.

Amen.

" I tell you, on the day of judgment people will give account for every careless word they speak, for by your words you will be justified, and by your words you will be condemned."

Matthew 12:36-37

"The cross stands both as God's ultimate warning of the consequences of sin, and as the greatest expression of His love for sinners."

Bryan Chapell

4

A Night to Remember

Daniel 5:1-6, 13-30

In returning to Daniel this morning, I bring up something I have not dealt with but which is of great importance—the reliability of this book. Daniel, as much as any other book, has become the subject of strong attacks by liberal scholars. One of the reasons has to do with the prophecies in the book that came true, such as the kingdom of the Medes and Persians, the prophecy concerning Jesus' birth and so forth. It is simply an argument from unbelief—prophecy is a miracle; miracles cannot happen; therefore, Daniel was not written until much later.

One reason for skepticism regarding Daniel has to do with Daniel 5, which we will read today. The charge is made that Nebuchadnezzar is called Belshazzar's father, but since other ancient literature clearly denies this, the Bible is wrong. Ancient extra-biblical writings revealed that there were three kings who succeeded Nebuchadnezzar "in rather rapid succession."[1] The last of these was a king named Nabonidus. Belshazzar was not even mentioned. Therefore, the skeptics charged that the Bible was wrong. But in 1854 a British counsel named J.G. Taylor was on a mission in southern Iraq for the British Museum and discovered several small cylinders inscribed with lines written, it said, by the command of Nabonidus containing a prayer for long life for his eldest son Belshazzar. "But!" the skeptic replies, "We now admit this, as well as several other archeological finds which mention Belshazzar as son of Nabonidus. However, Belshazzar is never mentioned as king!" True. But you should do your homework. Herodotus, the great Greek historian, tells us that Nabonidus went out to fight against Darius and was routed and fled to Borsippa where he was bottled up by Darius' troops. Darius then left that scene, with the king surrounded, and marched to take Babylon. In Daniel 5:16, the eccentric eldest

---
[1] James Montgomery Boice, *Daniel: An Expositional Commentary* (Grand Rapids, Michigan: Baker Books, 1989), 59.

son, Belshazzar, offers to make Daniel "the third ruler in the kingdom." Why the third? Because he was the second. His father was the true king. And so the Bible and the best of history and archeology now agree. As James Boice wrote:

> "If you want to look very wise in the world's eyes and are willing to risk looking foolish years from now, you can make a reputation for yourself by pointing out the 'errors' in the Bible."[2]

And so we come to one of the most dramatic events in world history, documented not only in the Bible, but established in history and in archeology. In Daniel we get an inside look at the last night of the existence of the Babylonian empire. But this is no mere story, no mere history. This is the inerrant and infallible Word of the living God written by God to glorify His Son and win our hearts back to Him.

> King Belshazzar made a great feast for a thousand of his lords and drank wine in front of the thousand. Belshazzar, when he tasted the wine, commanded that the vessels of gold and of silver that Nebuchadnezzar his father had taken out of the temple in Jerusalem be brought, that the king and his lords, his wives, and his concubines might drink from them. Then they brought in the golden vessels that had been taken out of the temple, the house of God in Jerusalem, and the king and his lords, his wives, and his concubines drank from them. They drank wine and praised the gods of gold and silver, bronze, iron, wood, and stone. Immediately the fingers of a human hand appeared and wrote on the plaster of the wall of the king's palace, opposite the lampstand. And the king saw the hand as it wrote. Then the king's color changed, and his thoughts alarmed him; his limbs gave way, and his knees knocked together (Daniel 5:1-6).
>
> Then Daniel was brought in before the king. The king answered and said to Daniel, "You are that Daniel, one of the exiles of Judah, whom the king my father brought from Judah. I have heard of you that the spirit of the gods is in you, and that light and understanding and excellent wisdom are found in you. Now the wise men, the enchanters, have been brought in before me to read this writing and make known to me its interpretation, but they could not show the interpretation of the matter. But I have heard that you can give interpretations and solve problems. Now if you can read the writing and make known to me its interpretation, you shall be clothed with purple and have a chain of gold around your neck and shall be the third ruler in the kingdom." Then Daniel answered and said before the king, "Let your gifts be for yourself, and give your rewards to another. Nevertheless, I will read

---

[2] Ibid., 60.

the writing to the king and make known to him the interpretation. O king, the Most High God gave Nebuchadnezzar your father kingship and greatness and glory and majesty. And because of the greatness that he gave him, all peoples, nations, and languages trembled and feared before him. Whom he would, he killed, and whom he would, he kept alive; whom he would, he raised up, and whom he would, he humbled. But when his heart was lifted up and his spirit was hardened so that he dealt proudly, he was brought down from his kingly throne, and his glory was taken from him. He was driven from among the children of mankind, and his mind was made like that of a beast, and his dwelling was with the wild donkeys. He was fed grass like an ox, and his body was wet with the dew of heaven, until he knew that the Most High God rules the kingdom of mankind and sets over it whom he will. And you his son, Belshazzar, have not humbled your heart, though you knew all this, but you have lifted up yourself against the Lord of heaven. And the vessels of his house have been brought in before you, and you and your lords, your wives, and your concubines have drunk wine from them. And you have praised the gods of silver and gold, of bronze, iron, wood, and stone, which do not see or hear or know, but the God in whose hand is your breath, and whose are all your ways, you have not honored. "Then from his presence the hand was sent, and this writing was inscribed. And this is the writing that was inscribed: MENE, MENE, TEKEL, and PARSIN. This is the interpretation of the matter: MENE, God has numbered the days of your kingdom and brought it to an end; TEKEL, you have been weighed in the balances and found wanting; PERES, your kingdom is divided and given to the Medes and Persians." Then Belshazzar gave the command, and Daniel was clothed with purple, a chain of gold was put around his neck, and a proclamation was made about him, that he should be the third ruler in the kingdom. That very night Belshazzar the Chaldean king was killed (Daniel 5:13-30).

BE PREPARED

It was a night to remember. Before James Cameron's blockbuster movie *Titanic*, the essential guide to what happened on that fateful night was—and I think remains—Walter Lord's 1955 classic *A Night to Remember*. Walter Lord uses eye witness accounts to reconstruct the tragedy that occurred on April 15, 1912, when human pride and foolish disregard for the possibility of calamity sailed into the treacherous iceberg fields of the North Atlantic. One reviewer of the book wrote,

> You share the early complacency of the passengers on the 'unsinkable' ship. Your sense of impending doom grows as the bows disappear below the glassy Atlantic. You grit your teeth at the obtuseness of the crew of the Californian—why, oh why, didn't they question those white rockets?—and you share in the breathless trauma of those on shore as the story unfolds.[3]

The message of that night remains etched in maritime history: however secure you may think you are, the consequences of complacency, with a force more powerful than man, will lead to sudden disaster. Be prepared. Make plans. Or it will be a night to remember for you!

It was a night to remember. Indeed it was a night I shall never forget. Youthful, fancy-free, a Friday night football game, a slight chill in the air, an after-game party for all the kids at the church's youth building, pulling up and seeing parents holding teenagers heaving tears, a chill running down my spine—these are the things I recall from that night. For on that night, a beautiful young girl, a girl named Marla, a girl I had grown up with, a girl I had been in school with and in Sunday school with, a girl who had begun to run around with the wrong crowd, was with that crowd in a car. The car took a curve on Highway 16 and went airborne. Marla was dead. And that night, all of our youthfulness and our supposed immortality went down like the *Titanic* beneath the cold Atlantic. Our imagined invincibility and the reckless abandonment and partying of one of our own met with a power greater than all of us, and she was gone. That night we were left, like survivors in a lifeboat, shivering from the power of sudden disaster, weeping from the pain of instant loss, and our blood running cold with the thought: We are not immortal after all; this could have been me.

It was a night to remember in Babylon. On October 13, 539 B.C., Babylon—invincible Babylon, the greatest empire the world had ever known—fell to the Medes and the Persians. Daniel and ancient history match perfectly, but the Bible tells us the rest of the story behind that fateful night. As Belshazzar held a drunken orgy, as the wine flowed freely, as pride swelled in the supposed impregnable fortress, as the foolish prince boasted in front of his thousand lords desecrating the sacred chalice stolen from the Temple of Jerusalem, as he mocked the God that his ancestor Nebuchadnezzar had come to worship as the Most High God, God crashed Belshazzar's party in a dramatic way. Daniel 5 reads like the Walter Lord first-hand account of the last hours of the *Titanic* but

---

[3] See the review at
http://www.amazon.com/exec/obidos/ASIN/0553278274/ref=ase_andrysbasten/103-40331 60-0647028 (accessed on October 1, 2004).

with shocking, even eerie events right out of an old Vincent Price movie—a disembodied hand writing on the wall of the palace and strange words being recorded, MENE, MENE, TEKEL, PARSIN.

Rather than just telling the bare facts of history, God let us in on this scene so that we could see the awful consequences of denying God. In his book *Standing Your Ground*, Bryan Chapell summed up the lesson of of Daniel 5,

> "Chapter five of Daniel becomes the flip-side of the previous one. In chapter four we learn that Daniel used King Nebuchadnezzar's conversion to affirm that the repentant reap the rewards of grace, however bleak their past. Now Daniel will use...Belshazzar's sacrilege to declare that the rebellious reap the consequences of wrath, however secure their present."[4]

It was, for all time, for all of mankind, and for all of our lives, a night to remember. Like the *Titanic*, like the tragic ending to a young life out of control, God compassionately calls us to prepare, to make plans, to make course adjustments in our lives lest we, too, come to face God's wrath against sin.

God crashed Belshazzar's idolatrous party in a mysterious way. There are two very clear lessons to take away from that night to remember.

Defiance of God Will Bring Judgment (Daniel 5:1-4)

In Daniel 5:1-4, Belshazzar's debaucherous party revealed his disregard for the responsibility he had been given. His father in the royal line, Nebuchadnezzar, had witnessed the power of God working through Daniel as well as the other three Hebrew lads. But Nebuchadnezzar's unbelief in the face of the clear testimony of God led the king to go crazy and eat grass like an ox. But God had mercy upon this pagan king, and Nebuchadnezzar turned to God and realized that there is only one sovereign Lord and that is God. But Belshazzar disregarded his own history.

In the Bible, the story of sin is the story of a disregard for the evidence of God that leads to severe judgment. Adam and Eve disregarded God's loving commands and were cast out of Eden. In Genesis 6, the people of the earth disregarded God's commandments for marriage, which led to violence in the earth and the earth was destroyed by the flood. We read that Eli the priest had sons who knew the things of God; yet, they did what was evil in God's sight, and

---

[4] Bryan Chapell, *Standing Your Ground: A Call to Courage in an Age of Compromise: Messages from Daniel* (Grand Rapids, Michigan: Baker Book House, 1989), 119-120.

God destroyed them. In Romans 1 Paul says that this is the cycle of sin at work in the world.

> For the wrath of God is revealed from heaven against all ungodliness and unrighteousness of men, who by their unrighteousness suppress the truth. For what can be known about God is plain to them, because God has shown it to them. For his invisible attributes, namely, his eternal power and divine nature, have been clearly perceived, ever since the creation of the world, in the things that have been made. So they are without excuse. For although they knew God, they did not honor him as God or give thanks to him, but they became futile in their thinking, and their foolish hearts were darkened. Claiming to be wise, they became fools, and exchanged the glory of the immortal God for images resembling mortal man and birds and animals and reptiles (Romans 1:18-23).

This is exactly what happened to Belshazzar. And on that night to remember, he was without excuse.

Today, many people in our churches have heard the Word of God preached week in and week out by faithful pastors. Many people across this nation have turned on radios and televisions and the Word of God has come to them. Many of our young people have been reared to learn Bible passages, study God's Word. But today, many have turned from the Lord. Like Belshazzar, they disregard the faith of their mothers and fathers. They have sought other gods. They have disregarded the great responsibility of the light they have been given. They are like Belshazzar—giving a party that they think will last forever. But the Bible says that God will not be mocked. And God says that unto whom much is given much is required.[5]

Since 1947 the *Bulletin of the Atomic Scientists* has told the world what time it is through an ominous sign they call the Doomsday Clock. This clock is set by their Board of Directors to alert the world to the dangers of destruction through nuclear war. After 9/11 the clock was reset from nine minutes until midnight to seven minutes until midnight, indicating their concerns.

On the night of Belshazzar's party, who would have thought that God had moved the hands on the Doomsday Clock for Babylon? The wine was flowing and the partying was at a pinnacle. But it was all about to come to an end. It would end because of disregard for the light God had given them.

---

[5] Luke 12:48

Every child of God who disregards the light of Christ stands, not in judgment, but stands to be severely disciplined by our Father. We are to make our calling and our election sure. If we persist in our secret sins against God, there is no palace, no fortress that can stop the hand of God. If you are listening to my voice and have heard the truth that there is a God, that He has spoken once and for all through His Son Jesus Christ, and if you do not avail yourself of the loving grace and compassion of Christ, if you disregard His sacrifice for your sins on Calvary, then my friend, you do not know where the hands of the clock of your life are at. It may be seven minutes until midnight. Or this could be the night to remember for you. But with one prayer, one moment of confession that you are a sinner in need of a Savior and that Jesus Christ is that Savior, you are saved and the clock stops forever.

That Judgment Is Spelled Out in God's Word
(Daniel 5:5-6, 24-28)

The depraved party, which included drunkenness and the sacrilege of consecrated vessels stolen in times past from the Temple of Jerusalem, came to a sudden end with disembodied fingers on a hand writing on the plaster of the palace, opposite the lampstand. God didn't want anyone to miss it. God gave light for them to see this amazing event. Daniel was called in and promised the attire of royalty and offered the third place in the kingdom if he could interpret it. Daniel told the king to give the rewards to someone else. Daniel worked for God alone. Daniel interpreted the writing on the wall. MENE, MENE, TEKEL, PARSIN are Aramaic derivatives.

> MENE means, God has numbered your days and brought it to an end. This is repeated for emphasis.
>
> TEKEL means, you have been weighed on the scales and found wanting.
>
> PERES (singular of PARSIN) means, God has divided your kingdom and it is given to Persia.

Now let's consider all of this together. We know what it said to Belshazzar, but what do the fingers of heaven, the writing on the wall, and the interpretation of Daniel mean to us?

God's Word is a "Word from Another World"

The Word comes in a startling, out-of-this-world way: disembodied fingers spelling out judgment on a wall for all to see. I have said before that the book of

Daniel, like other parts of the Word of God, is derided as containing error. But the pride of man is always lowered by the very manner in which God's Word comes. God's Word came without human aid, in a mysterious way, to reveal God's truth to Belshazzar. God's Word is miraculous. God's Word is, as my old professor used to say, "a word from another world."[6] The best thing we can do in our culture is to preach and teach the Word of God. It is supernatural, and the power of that Word will work with the Spirit that inspired it to open up the hearts of the lost, cause straying believers to return to the fold, and when necessary, convict the world of sin as well as of the righteousness needed to stand before Almighty God. The book of Hebrews records,

> how shall we escape if we neglect such a great salvation? It was declared at first by the Lord, and it was attested to us by those who heard, while God also bore witness by signs and wonders and various miracles and by gifts of the Holy Spirit distributed according to his will (Hebrews 2:3-4).

The Word of God came through fingers writing on the wall at a party. At another time God's finger scribbled in the sand, and a woman who was caught in adultery was forgiven, and those who thought they were secure in their own righteousness were condemned. God has scribbled onto history with His Word. And the supernatural power of what God writes on our hearts through the Spirit inspired Word from another world is intended to show us our true condition and cause us to repent and turn to Him.

God's Word is a Word that we can understand

The doctrine of the perspicuity of Scripture means that man can understand the Word of God. Though the message was foreign to the pagan Belshazzar, it was known by Daniel and preached to Belshazzar. The spiritual things of God cannot be discerned by unbelievers, and until God interrupts our sinful lives with His surprising presence, we do not take notice. But the message is clear. The message itself is the message contained in the Word of God from beginning to end. Mene, Mene, Tekel, Parsin is the beginning of the gospel truth: Man without God is under the condemnation of God. Our works have been weighed and found wanting. The labors of our hands, the best intentions of our hearts, are yet laced with sin. A little sin poisons the whole lump. Our days, likewise, are numbered. There will come an end to our days and we will stand before a holy God. This message is not intended to scare us anymore than a sign telling us that a bridge is out is intended to scare us. It is intended to steer us to safety. And the only safety, the only ark of our salvation is the Lord Jesus Christ.

---

[6] Dr. Robert L. Reymond

God's Word Is a Word That Must be Taught by Faithful Disciples

God could have spoken directly to Belshazzar, but He spoke through His faithful disciple, Daniel. Paul wrote in Romans,

> But how are they to call on him in whom they have not believed? And how are they to believe in him of whom they have never heard? And how are they to hear without someone preaching? And how are they to preach unless they are sent? As it is written, "How beautiful are the feet of those who preach the good news!" (Romans 10:14-15).

Daniel came preaching and teaching the Word of God as it came in signs and wonders. John the Baptist came preaching repentance for the coming Christ. And the Bible says that Jesus came preaching that the kingdom of God was at hand.

The work of the church—of our church, beloved—is to declare the Word of the Lord: Man is in sin. God will judge sin. But God judged sin when He judged His only Son. And whoever believes in Him is forgiven and all things become new.

As Daniel cared not for the offers of Belshazzar's wealth, the church must not be bribed by offers of power or influence. We do our work best when we focus on our message: Repent or perish. Believe in Christ and be saved. Receive the forgiveness of God in Christ and live life beyond the limits.

From "A Night to Remember" to "A Day Like No Other"

I want to move now from a night to remember to a day like no other. That day was the day when the Lord reached down again from heaven, interrupted the rebellion of man in this world, and out of love, sent His Son Jesus. It was a day like no other for, again, God broke through our isolation and our pride and our supposed fortress to come as a baby to a virgin. I admit that a feed trough isn't as frightening as disembodied fingers, but it should get your attention. Angels singing in the heavens and Christ born in the city of David, exactly when and how the Old Testament said it would happen, also makes this a day like no other. And it was a day like no other when this Jesus grew and when He was baptized, and again, God's power broke through and declared, "This is my beloved son with whom I am well pleased"[7] There were many other such days—days when God reached down through the closed doors of blindness or deafness or spoke to demons and healed tormented souls. And then there was

---
[7] Matthew 3:17

the day like no other when God broke through to every Belshazzar in the world and gave Himself up to be crucified. When all other divine breakthroughs stopped—no angels descending to rescue him from the hands of evil, no angelic hand to stop the instrument that would slaughter the sacrificial lamb. God was there but was covered in blood and drooping in death. The earth would convulse in darkness and earthquakes at the sight. Then in three days there would be another day like no other when Jesus of Nazareth would rise from the dead. He would be seen by over five hundred at once. There would be many more days like no other. There would be a day when a man named Saul would have his palace invaded, his life startled by the risen Christ, and he would never be the same. There would be a day like no other when a failed missionary and a heartbroken young man named John Wesley would come to see that he could have in his own life what Luther had written: assurance of eternal life. And on a street called Aldersgate, John Wesley described what happened as "I felt my heart strangely warmed."

It was a day like no other day when I froze with fear—when I felt that God was in that room and in my heart—and His finger scribbled out the words on my soul:

> For by grace are ye saved through faith; and that not of yourselves: it is the gift of God: Not of works, lest any man should boast (Ephesians 2:8-9, KJV).

And life has never been the same. From a night to remember and a day like no other, let us conclude with what we now face this moment.

A Time That May Never Come Again

A night to remember was when God's Word came to judge Man's sin. A day like no other was when God's Son came to take man's judgment. But there is also a time that may never come again…and that time is right now. The book of Daniel is not just a book of history, it is the living Word of God coming not only to Belshazzar, but also to you. Perhaps from this message you now know that the Holy Spirit reaches into your life to reveal your true condition for facing judgment without Christ. Today is the day to look to Jesus Christ and say, "Lord, this old party is over. I've thrown away the idols. I have read the writing on my heart plainly. I am a sinner. I need a Savior. That Savior is the One Daniel wrote about and the One I pray about—the Lord Jesus Christ. I receive and rest upon Him alone—His life, His death, His resurrection, His Word. Please forgive me."

And He will. And the great thing about following the Lord is that you learn what a real party is all about. Life in Christ may not always be easy, but it beats what happened to Belshazaar anytime. Life in Christ is not Belshazzar's drunken party, but our festive picnic, filled with laughter and singing and children running around and fellowship with old friends and new friends. People with one thing in common—we have all read the writing plainly, and we have turned to Jesus Christ. Today is the day for you.

The Bible says,

> ...Behold, now is the day of salvation (2 Corinthians 6:2b).

Questions for Reflection

1. What have been some of the "nights to remember" in our lives? What were the effects of these momentous events in your life? In the life of the nation? How was God glorified through these events?

2. Do you see any way in which we, as a nation, have abandoned a heritage of faith given to us by our forefathers? How about in your own family? Think through the implications of disregarding a heritage of faith in Christ and what it can do to a nation, or a family, or an individual.

3. Taking a long view of Scripture, how does God spell out His will for us today? How do we teach the Bible to people who do not believe it or do not believe it to be inerrant and infallible?

4. Are you a first generation believer? A second? Third or more? Do you know and could you relate the "Aldersgate Road" experience of your life or the life of the one who introduced true faith in Christ into your family? How is cherishing this and retelling this event a blessing to families? How do we relate our testimonies when we are reared in a Christian home and receive the faith of our parents as our own without cataclysmic personal failure? Can these testimonies be just as effective? If so, how?

Prayer

Lord of life, You reached down to a world in crisis through Christ and through the continuing testimony of Your Word and Your Spirit. Reach down this very moment and stir up fresh faith in Jesus Christ in my life. Cause me to love Your gospel and give me boldness to tell this old, old story of Your love to my family and to those who have never heard. For the sake of Jesus Christ my Lord.

Amen.

"Those who turn many to righteousness, who turn sinners from the errors of their ways, and help to save their souls from death ... will share in the glory of those they have helped to heaven, which will add to their own glory."

Matthew Henry

"No one of God's children ought to confine their attention privately to themselves, but as far as possible, every one ought to interest himself in the welfare of his brethren. God has deposited the teaching of His salvation with us, not for the purpose of our privately keeping it to ourselves, but of our pointing out the way of salvation to all mankind."

John Calvin

5

THE RELATIONSHIP OF PROPHECY AND MISSIONS

Daniel 12:1-4; Acts 1:6-11

Today I want to move through Daniel 7-11 to come to the powerful conclusion of this great book. Moving through Daniel 7-11 in a matter of a few moments to get to the majestic statement of Daniel 12 is sort of like the time Mae and I ran arrived at the Louvre in Paris fifteen minutes before closing. We literally ran past Reubens, Van Goghs and Raphaels. But we were running to something great: Leonardo's *Mona Lisa*!

And running past these chapters is admittedly running past masterpieces of prophecy! I hope by God's grace to return to this divine gallery at some other time. But where we are going this morning will bring us to the serene, smiling portrait of all prophecy. It is the sum of all prophecy.

> "At that time shall arise Michael, the great prince who has charge of your people. And there shall be a time of trouble, such as never has been since there was a nation till that time. But at that time your people shall be delivered, everyone whose name shall be found written in the book. And many of those who sleep in the dust of the earth shall awake, some to everlasting life, and some to shame and everlasting contempt. And those who are wise shall shine like the brightness of the sky above; and those who turn many to righteousness, like the stars forever and ever. But you, Daniel, shut up the words and seal the book, until the time of the end. Many shall run to and fro, and knowledge shall increase." (Daniel 12:1-4)
>
> Now in these days when the disciples were increasing in number, a complaint by the Hellenists arose against the Hebrews because their widows were being neglected in the daily distribution. And the twelve summoned the full number of the disciples and said, "It is not right that we should give

up preaching the word of God to serve tables. Therefore, brothers, pick out from among you seven men of good repute, full of the Spirit and of wisdom, whom we will appoint to this duty. But we will devote ourselves to prayer and to the ministry of the word." And what they said pleased the whole gathering, and they chose Stephen, a man full of faith and of the Holy Spirit, and Philip, and Prochorus, and Nicanor, and Timon, and Parmenas, and Nicolaus, a proselyte of Antioch. These they set before the apostles, and they prayed and laid their hands on them. And the word of God continued to increase, and the number of the disciples multiplied greatly in Jerusalem, and a great many of the priests became obedient to the faith. And Stephen, full of grace and power, was doing great wonders and signs among the people. Then some of those who belonged to the synagogue of the Freedmen (as it was called), and of the Cyrenians, and of the Alexandrians, and of those from Cilicia and Asia, rose up and disputed with Stephen. But they could not withstand the wisdom and the Spirit with which he was speaking. Then they secretly instigated men who said, "We have heard him speak blasphemous words against Moses and God." (Acts 6:1-11)

The Way Out of the Swamp

I will never forget getting lost in a swamp down in Louisiana when I was a boy. Everywhere I looked there were possible passages through the moss hanging off the water oaks; through the low hanging cypress limbs; across the black, brown, and green gumbo water. But which one to take? The more I concentrated on getting out of the swamp, the deeper into it I got!

Upon coming to the prophecies in Daniel 9, one old trusted interpreter warned,

> Interpreters should hesitate before entering afresh into the exegesis of Daniel's seventy weeks, a passage that has been characterized as "the Dismal Swamp of Old Testament criticism."[1]

Another great commentator, E.J. Young, one of the greats of Westminster Seminary, wrote,

> ...the termination of the 70 sevens coincides with... the first advent of our Lord.[2]

And Robert D. Culver of Trinity Evangelical Seminary, has written that it is to be fulfilled

---

[1] J. Barton Payne, "The Goal of Daniel's Seventy Weeks," *The Journal of the Evangelical Theological Society 21*, no. 2 (1978).
[2] Ibid.

...no earlier than the coming of Christ at the second advent.[3]

So, men of good will, yes, even Bible-believing scholars of untouchable reputations, can disagree. But is there a way out of the swamp?

The prophecies of Daniel 7-11 contain visions, like the one in Daniel 2, which interpret Daniel's days by showing the continual rise and fall of nations until the appearance of the Messiah and then of the consummation of the ages. The prophecies are nothing short of amazing. For instance, in Daniel 9, Daniel (by this time he is over ninety years of age) is studying prophecy himself. He studies Jeremiah's prophecy about the seventy years of captivity in Babylon. He recognizes that the time is near for the judgment to be over. So the old man, Daniel, prays, fasts, and does several things:

- He confesses God's covenant faithfulness (Daniel 9:4)
- He confesses Israel's sin (Daniel 9:5)
- He seeks God's righteousness (Daniel 9:7)
- He seeks God's atonement for sin (Daniel 9:16)

As Daniel prays, God wastes no time in answering. God answers through Gabriel, who later announces the birth of Jesus. In Daniel 9:24-27 the Lord gives Daniel his answer.

The passage, following on Daniel's insight into the seventy-year judgment prophesied by Jeremiah, introduces a prophecy that after the decree to rebuild Jerusalem, there will be seventy weeks or units of sevens (70 x 7 weeks of years or 490 years).[4] Following perfectly with Daniel's prayer, the revelation deals with putting an end to the judgment, to atone for iniquity, to bring in everlasting righteousness. Matthew Henry said of these passages,

> We have, in verses 24-27, one of the most undeniable prophecies of Christ, of his coming and his salvation.[5]

But having pointed to the greater prophetic meaning, Matthew Henry also said,

> There are indeed difficulties in expounding this passage, which have occasioned different opinions among commentators...[6]

---

[3] Ibid.
[4] "This verse sets forth the approach of 'seventy "sevens"' of years during which God would accomplish his plan...The seventy 'weeks' or 'heptads' (*sabuim* literally means 'units of seven,' whether days or years) are 490 years (divided, as we shall see, into three sections)." Gleason Archer, "Daniel" in Frank E. Gaebelein, ed, *The Expositor's Bible Commentary*, vol 7 (Grand Rapids, Michigan: Zondervan Publishing House, 1985), 112.
[5] Matthew Henry and Thomas Scott, *Commentary on the Holy Bible*, vol. II (Nashville, Tennessee: Thomas Nelson, 1979).
[6] Ibid.

Without going into the several interpretations, we can say what most say: This passage looks forward 490 years from the decree of Artixerxes I to the crucifixion of Jesus Christ. In Him, all of the promises are fulfilled. Now there are several other things that could be said and should be studied about the meaning of these prophecies, but it is possible to get so focused on trying to break the codes on these apocalyptic passages that we miss the larger truths they are teaching. That is where we get lost in the swamp.

I spent over five years studying the swampy waters of seventeenth century Puritanism which led to the tremendous problems in British Christianity in that day. Perhaps you would like me to put you to sleep one night with my research! At the heart of it was a man who exemplified the problem. Vavasor Powell was called of God to preach the gospel. He spent his first few years doing just that. In fact, he was sent out by the Westminster Assembly to reform the church in Wales, which was still backward and even superstitious in many ways. He went about his work with success. But eventually he was captivated by some of the prophecies we have talked about this morning. He got into a movement called The Fifth Monarchy movement, which believed that the four monarchies, or kingdoms, of Daniel were fulfilled and that the final kingdom was about to come. It was the 1640s. All of the old institutions were crumbling. The Church of England was no more. The government was in shambles. Charles I would be beheaded in 1649. Anarchy was spreading like cancer with groups like the Levelers who believed that prophecy demanded that all authorities be overthrown to make way for Christ's return. A civil war, largely over the interpretation of Scripture, was spilling the blood of brother against brother. Meanwhile, the economy was in shambles. All of this was happening while England watched the bloody Thirty Year War ravaging Europe, tearing down monarchies and rearranging the political map. Vavasor Powell and many of his contemporaries begin to be obsessed with trying to calculate all of the numbers in Daniel's prophecies by the events of their day. More and more they began to focus their ministries on trying to break the code. In doing so, they left their parishes. They formed study groups, not to study God's grace and how to share it with others, not to promote missions, not to be about the work that Jesus told us we must do, but they stood looking into the heavens, trying to link each and every world event to prophecy. In the end, these who had opposed the king as standing in the way of the coming of Christ, which they thought would be in 1666, opposed each other. On the day that Oliver Cromwell would be made Lord Protector, Vavasor Powell would preach in Blackfriars Church and ask his congregation, "Will you have Jesus to rule over you or Oliver Cromwell." Of course, he was locked up by Cromwell. For all practical purposes, his ministry was over. By focusing on prophecy as a study unto itself rather than as a means to call him to evangelize others while there was still time, he forfeited his pastoral ministry.[7] They were lost in the prophecy swamp, and every calculation and every attempt to reconcile numbers and images of beasts and kingdoms with newspaper headlines led them deeper and deeper away from the light.

There have been many Vavasor Powells since then. The fields of church history are littered with sad stories of well-intentioned groups that have been started by suspending the ordinary work of the gospel in order to sit on mountaintops and wait for Christ to return. There are conferences abounding that focus, not on the ordinary work of following the Lord in our lives, of fulfilling the Great Commission, but on trying to link every headline in the newspaper with a prophecy in the Bible. The problem is not that prophecy should not be studied or that we should not read the signs of our times, but that we are charged by Christ to be about preaching the gospel.

So this leads to a question, How do we get out of the swamp? What is the relationship between these prophecies and the work of the church?

People who get lost in the swamp have lost their way because they veered away from the purpose of their trip. You get out by following the light that led you in. You get out of the swamp of murky interpretation by looking to the Light of Men, the Lord Jesus Christ. In arriving at Daniel 12, we come to the light. In Daniel 12, the Lord shows every believer about the relationship of the prophecies to the great work of the church in this world. This relationship of prophecy and the work of the church may be seen in five certainties and in one challenge.

Five Certainties

The times are determined (Daniel 12:1a: "At that time...")

Daniel 12 begins with a reference to the great enemy of the Lord in Daniel 11. But what is also clear is that there is a time set to deal with him. Time is not running away like a stray cat. Time is under the control of God. The years are on a leash. This is for certain. All can agree with this. This is the summary of the matter. God is sovereign and in control. Our days are numbered. The days of

---

[7] See Michael A. Milton, "The Pastoral Predicament of Vavasor Powell (1617-1670): Eschatological Fervor and Its Relationship to the Pastoral Ministry," *The Journal of the Evangelical Theological Society* 43, no. 3 (2000).

the earth are numbered. Nebuchadnezzar learned that God alone is sovereign and Nebuchadnezzar would testify,

> ...he does according to His will (Daniel 4:35)

God has a plan, and no man and no nation can stop it. Alexander the Great's days were numbered. Rome's days were numbered. Napoleon's days were numbered. Hitler's days were numbered. My days are numbered. And the earth's days are numbered.

Peter said that while the scoffers say that things will go on as always, just like they did in the days of Noah, the truth is that Christ is coming again and time will be no more. The earth and the cosmos itself will be destroyed and there will be a new heaven and a new earth.[8] Jesus said the timing for these things is not revealed to us. It is for the Father to know. Why? Because we are to be about the work God has given us to do. We are to be about growing in God's grace and then sharing that grace with others. The days are numbered and God will take care of God's business. It is enough for me to study Daniel and see that time will not go on forever.

The saints are defended (Daniel 12:1b, NKJV: "...Michael shall stand up, The great prince who stands watch over the sons of your people...")

In the Bible, Michael stands up for God's people. Michael is identified here as the great prince of angels in charge of God's people. We read about Michael in two places:

> But when the archangel Michael, contending with the devil, was disputing about the body of Moses, he did not presume to pronounce a blasphemous judgment, but said, "The Lord rebuke you" (Jude 1:9).

> Now war arose in heaven, Michael and his angels fighting against the dragon. And the dragon and his angels fought back, (Revelation 12:7).

In prophecy, then, we learn that God defends us. God has sent angels to guard over His people. Daniel and his people in Babylon were under captivity, but God had an angel guarding them. When ancient Israel was under the attack of mad kings, God defended them. When Mary and Joseph were in that manger and Herod turned against them, God defended them. When Paul preached the gospel, God defended them. And God is with you. Three times when Daniel sees trouble brewing against his people in the visions, we hear the Word of God saying to Him,

---

[8] 2 Peter 3

> ... you are greatly loved...(Daniel 9:23).
>
> ..."O Daniel, man greatly loved...(Daniel 10:11).
>
> And he said, "O man greatly loved, fear not, peace be with you; be strong and of good courage." And as he spoke to me, I was strengthened and said, "Let my lord speak, for you have strengthened me" (Daniel 10:19).

Today God wants you to know that the force of all prophecy is for you not to fear but to know that you are loved and that you are defended. There may be many other differences in prophetic understanding, but we can all agree with the hymn of Martin Luther:

> And though this world, with devils filled,
> should threaten to undo us,
> We will not fear, for God hath willed
> His truth to triumph thro' us:
> The Prince of Darkness grim,
> we tremble not for him;
> His rage we can endure,
> for lo, his doom is sure,
> One little word shall fell him.

The world will decline (Daniel 12:1c, NKJV: "...And there shall be a time of trouble, such as never was sine there was a nation, even to that time.")

In Matthew 24, Jesus said,

> "For then there will be great tribulation, such as has not been from the beginning of the world until now, no, and never will be. And if those days had not been cut short, no human being would be saved. But for the sake of the elect those days will be cut short" (Matthew 24:21-22).

We may anticipate a worsening of the conditions of mankind upon the earth. But we may also recognize the truth that Jesus taught—the kingdom of Christ will also continue to grow. What started as a mustard seed will end up as a giant tree. What began as a little leavening in the lump will be worked through to take over the whole lump. To dismiss the growth of the kingdom would be to deny these teachings, but to dismiss the growth of evil in the world would be to deny the teaching here and in other places. So we have a simultaneous growth of good and evil. But with God, where sin abounds grace abounds more.

Believers will be delivered (Daniel 12:1d, NKJV: "And at that time your people shall be delivered...")

In all prophetic interpretation there is the truth that the tribulation of God's people will not last forever. Christ will intervene.

At the breakfast table, this past week, Mae read the account of a little girl in Kansas City who had been suffering with cancer. She was dying. She was suffering terribly. And so she said, "Mother will you do something for me?" The mother said, "Of course." The little girl wanted her to know that this was very serious. Her mother said, "I will do whatever you want." The little girl said, "I want to go." She was asking permission of her mother to let her die and so be released from her suffering.

Beloved, the truth of God's Word is that we, too, no matter what kind of tribulation we face, will be delivered by the Lord. I have seen it in small ways in suffering. And this teaches us that in great tribulation, there is also a time of deliverance.

But we see that this is not given to all.

Mankind is divided (Daniel 12:1e-2, NKJV: "Every one who is found written in the book. And many of those who sleep in the dust of the earth shall awake, some to everlasting life, some to shame and everlasting contempt")

Mankind is divided between those whose names are in the book of life and those whose names are not. This book of life was recognized by Jesus when he said,

> "... rejoice that your names are written in heaven" (Luke 10:20, NIV)

Paul wrote of this in Philippians when he wrote about

> ... my fellow workers, whose names are in the book of life (Philippians 4:3, NIV)

Revelation speaks of the book of life six times. One famous passage declares,

> And I saw the dead, great and small, standing before the throne, and books were opened. Another book was opened, which is the book of life. And the dead were judged according to what they had done as recorded in the books (Revelation 20:12, NIV).

So prophecy teaches us that those who have turned from themselves to trusting in Christ have their names in His book of life.

It also teaches us something wondrous:

> And many of those who sleep in the dust of the earth shall awake, some to everlasting life, some to shame and everlasting contempt (Daniel 12:2).

There is coming a day of resurrection of all who have ever lived on this earth. Our spirits will have been judged at the very moment of our deaths, reserved either in the presence of the Lord Jesus or in hell. But on the day when Christ comes again, He will judge the living and the dead. Those spirits with Christ shall return with him and by caught up, body and soul. Those in hell shall be summoned from that awful place to also stand, body and soul, before the Almighty. On that day, those whose names are not found in the book of life, who have not trusted in Jesus Christ, will be sentenced to what Revelation calls a second death. Daniel calls it "shame and everlasting contempt." This is the final judgment of eternal separation from God, the final judgment of hell. But those whose names are in the book of life will be given everlasting life with the Lord Himself. The old African-American spiritual was both theologically and biblically accurate and poetic when it says,

> My Lord, what a morning!
> My Lord, what a morning!
> O my Lord, what a morning!
> When the stars begin to fall.
>
> You'll hear a sinner mourn,
> To wake the nations underground,
> Looking to my God's right hand,
> When the stars begin to fall.
>
> You'll hear a Christian sing,
> To wake the nations underground,
> Looking to my God's right hand,
> When the stars begin to fall.
>
> My Lord, what a morning!
> My Lord, what a morning!
> O my Lord, what a morning!
> When the stars begin to fall.

So men of good will may differ on many things. Daniel himself could not have imagined all that he saw and did not understand it all. But Daniel 12 leads us to agree on five certainties of prophecy:

- The days are determined
- The saints are defended
- The world will decline
- Believers will be delivered
- Mankind is divided

But where do we go with this? What shall we do with prophecy? Daniel is given a challenge.

One challenge

> Those who are wise shall shine like the brightness of the firmament, and those who turn many to righteousness like the stars forever and ever (Daniel 12:3)

The word for wise here is the word *sakal*. It means to have gained insight and understanding. You see, prophecy should lead us to a new insight and that insight, that wisdom, that understanding is this:

If our days are numbered and God alone knows the day when Christ will return, when the day of resurrection and judgment will happen, then we must be about the work of turning many to righteousness. The only righteousness, the only thing that can write our names in the book of life, is the righteousness of our Lord Jesus Christ, who is the figure in and through all of Daniel. The Son of man reigns over all of history and is calling His people to share Christ in every circumstance, to every king, to every people. Kings and kingdoms rise and fall. We may find ourselves now under Nebuchadnezzar, now under Belteshazzar, now under Darius, now under the Greeks or the Romans or in twenty-first century America. But wherever we are, it is our time to point others to the only sovereign of the universe, Jesus Christ. And for those who do, they will shine like the sun.

The other morning I went out early. The stars were still out. I was thinking about this passage and thinking about the heroes of the faith that my family and I had been reading about in family worship. I looked up into the sky and thought about these things. I thought about how there were some great ones who had shared Christ who are now reflecting the glory of Jesus Christ back to Him in heaven, which is what I think this means. In that great constellation of witnesses for the Lord, there is Daniel, now shining like a star in the presence of Jesus, for he turned many to righteousness in his day. Paul is shining like a star, for he turned many to righteousness in his day. There is Augustine in the eastern sky, shining for all of the souls he turned to Christ. There in the northern sky is Luther. There in the western sky, Martin Lloyd-Jones with his Welsh miners who were led to Christ by the Doctor. I have seen my Aunt Eva lead people to Christ in our living room, and I know she is shining like a star for she turned many to righteousness. I wondered about my life, my time. When my Aunt Eva died, she pulled me close. She did not say anything about my studies, my interpretation of prophecy, or my eschatological position. At that moment, we knew only the essentials. God is in control. Time is marching on, but it will one day, like her life, come to an end. No, she did not quiz me on the details. She just said, "Keep up the good work [of the gospel]." She was saying, "Be wise. Turn others to Christ. Come shine."

And thinking on these things, I ask myself, Does my theology lead me to marvel at the study? Or does it lead me to weep for the nations? Does my Bible study cause me to enter into controversial discussions and church splits over when this or that will happen and how? Or does my Bible lead me to stop looking *into* the heavens and start looking for people to join me in heaven?"

> ..."It is not for you to know times or seasons that the Father has fixed by His own authority...but you will be my witness in Jerusalem, and in all Judea, and Samaria, and to the end of the earth" (Acts 1:7-8)

The goal of prophecy and the demand of discipleship is to know the Lord Jesus Christ and to make Him known to others in the time God has given us.

Beloved, let us not waver from sharing Christ today. For when we do, we are promised to shine tomorrow.

Questions for Reflection

1. How is prophecy related to discipleship in Daniel?

2. Do you believe that it is possible to allow prophecy to overwhelm the life of discipleship in a believer's life? How? What dangers are there for ignoring it? How does ignoring prophecy impact our daily walk with the Lord?

3. How do the five "certainties" of prophecy suggested here impact world missions? Take each one of the five certainties (Refer to page 73).

THE RELATIONSHIP OF PROPHECY AND MISSIONS   CHAPTER 5

4. How do you see grace abounding in godless times? Is there evidence of it in your own life and circumstances?

5. How does your theology lead you to humility? To brokenheartedness for the lost? How is your theology related to what God is doing in the world today?

Prayer

O Sovereign Lord, Your Word is always practical, lively, and leading us to Your will. Guard my mind against any study that leads me to speculation rather than faith. Create a missions mind and a missions heart in my life, O Lord. Help me to live out Your Word through compassionate outreach and never through isolated intellectualism. Forgive me if I have ever kept Your Word for myself and not shared it. Help me to be faithful in these days and to be an encourager of faith in others. Through Christ our risen and reigning Lord, I pray.

Amen.

Michael A. Milton

In 2001, Dr. Michael A. Milton was called as the pastor of the historic First Presbyterian Church of Chattanooga, Tennessee, the twelfth in 161 years. As senior pastor, he provides expository preaching, teaching, and worship leadership to a growing congregation of over 2,000. He also serves as staff leader to pastors, directors, and hundreds of volunteers in a multi-faceted ministry that includes a radio and television outreach, a vibrant departmental Sunday School ministry, an aggressive world missions program, a camping ministry, and an outreach to the nation through numerous local and national agencies and ministries.

He can be heard on the *Faith for Living with Mike Milton* radio ministry in select regional markets of the United States and on the Internet at 1stpresbyterian.com. Dr. Milton is the author of the book *Leaving a Career to Follow a Call: A Vocational Guide to the Ordained Ministry*, as well as numerous popular and academic articles and published sermons in such periodicals as *Preaching Magazine*, *The Journal of the Evangelical Theological Society*, *The Christian Observer*, and *World Magazine*. He has been featured on national radio and television programs such as *Truths that Transform* with Dr. D. James Kennedy, *The Coral Ridge Hour*, and Moody Radio's *Money Matters*.

Prior to becoming Senior Pastor at First Presbyterian Church of Chattanooga, Dr. Milton served sixteen years in the business world and was also a top secret Navy linguist. He interned under D. James Kennedy at Coral Ridge Presbyterian Church and after seminary, planted two churches: Redeemer Presbyterian Church in Overland Park, Kansas; and Kirk O' the Isles Church in Savannah, Georgia. He also founded Westminster Academy Christian School in Overland Park and was the administrative head and a professor at Knox Theological Seminary. A graduate of Mid America Nazarene University (Kansas) and Knox Theological Seminary, in 1998 he earned a Doctor of Philosophy degree in theology and religious studies from The University of Wales (UK).

Dr. Milton's personal story of moving from orphan and prodigal son to understanding God's grace and receiving His adoption through Jesus Christ forms a frequent motif for offering Christ's healing to a broken generation. Often his sermons are illustrated with songs that he writes, sings, and performs with guitar.

In addition to his pastoral work, Dr. Milton holds a commission in the US Army Reserves as a chaplain, a ministry that he continues. Serving on several boards and active in a number of civic organizations, he also remains involved in preaching and teaching in churches, conferences, and seminaries. Mae and Mike are the parents of seven adult children and live with their ten-year-old son, John Michael, on Signal Mountain, Tennessee, where they are frequently found puttering in the garden.

www.ingramcontent.com/pod-product-compliance
Lightning Source LLC
Chambersburg PA
CBHW072011090426
42734CB00033B/2439